DON'T WAIT, MAKE THINGS HAPPEN

TWELVE ATTRIBUTES OF AN EFFECTIVE PERSONALITY

Dr SURESH CHARI

ISBN 979-8-88815-650-6

Contents

Dr Vedprakash Mishra
Pro-Chancellor

Datta Meghe Institute of Medical Sciences (Deemed to be University)

Foreword

The paradigm shift in the domain of personality development and teaching-learning approach and process has to be in terms of the entire modality getting altered to be 'learner centric' rather than operationally turning out to be 'teacher centric'. It is towards the fulfilment of this desired shift—it is desirable, not imperative—that the entire learning turns out to be not only pleasurable but also has to be joyous as well. It must result in the learner not only getting into the mode of understanding what is taught to him but also beingcapable of grasping and articulating it in a handy and free-flowing manner without any hindrances inter alia barriers of any type.

In order to achieve this vital target which ultimately turns out to be the soul of the entire desired process totally conducive to the learner in facilitating his optimal learning, the important and core parts of the book *Don't wait, make things happen* has to be appropriately viewed in the form of facilitatory, learning resource material in the truest sense. This aspect to my understanding would stand accomplished in the form of a book embodying the desired inclusions so as to ensure fulfilment of the targeted objective in the context of it being conducive to learning and understanding critically the contours of personality making articulately.

The information and the contents therein definitely would be handy and of referral consequence to all the stakeholders. The core dispensation that is required to be achieved out of such creation is to make all the stakeholders aware of all the relevant details in terms of its operability and demonstrability as well so that it can be availed for the desired transformation of the user.

The compilation of such magnitude is not an ordinary and mundane task. It means and mandates diligent application of mind and sincere efforts put in for meaningful actualisation of the same.

As such, the initiative that has been worked out by Dr Suresh Chari in this context is not only laudable but in my opinion, would go a long way in catering to the larger cause of not only facilitating the much-desired issue of personality development of the young generation in a cogent and credible manner but would also result in the fulfilment of the legitimately desired expectations of the youth.

The entire perspective against which the creative work of Dr Suresh Chari needs to be viewed in my opinion is the dictum professed by Late Dr Abdul Kalam, "Just as the 19th century belonged to Britishers, the 20th century belonged to Americans, in the same vein 21st century will belong to Indians. This is possible exclusively when the demographic dividends that India as a country has within its fold aretransformed into precious human resources. It is this transformation resulting in the generation of effectively trained and tuned manpower which is the roadmap to the Global Supremacy of Mother India."

It is in this domain that the creative generation of Dr Suresh Chari would be acting as a huge catalyst in the transformation of the demographic dividends into precious human resources in terms of the creation of a personality from a person resulting in his or her conversion into a persona.

Yours Sincerely,

Professor of Excellence, Professor of Eminence,

Professor Emeritus and Distinguished Professor,

Dr Vedprakash Mishra

Dr B. C. Roy National Awardee,

D.Sc. (Honoris Causa) by Seven Universities

National Head of the Academic Programme of Indian Programme UNESCO Chair in Bio-Ethics Haifa & Member of the International Committee for Bioethics for Asia Pacific Region

Chief Advisor to Hon'ble Chancellor and Krishna Institute of Medical Sciences (Deemed to be University), Karad

Pro-Chancellor, Datta Meghe Institute of Medical Sciences (Deemed to be University), Nagpur

Advisor, Human Ethics Committees Association (HECA), Bangalore

Dean, Academic and Accreditation Board, National Indian Medical Association, New Delhi

Honorary Professor, Indian Medical Association

Honorary Director, Centre for Health Sciences Education Policy and Planning, DMIMS(DU), Nagpur

Former Vice Chancellor, Datta Meghe Institute of Medical Sciences (Deemed University), Nagpur

Former Chairman, Postgraduate Medical Education Committee, Medical Council of India, New Delhi

Former Chairman, Academic Council, Medical Council of India, New Delhi

Foreword

Someone aptly observed a few years ago that there's a deluge of self-help books, spiritual gibberish and books on mushy love. So very true. Sifting through them and zeroing in on a book that can be called the cat's whiskers is a veritable uphill task. Yet, once in a blue moon, you chance upon a book that makes you exclaim, **Eureka**! Suresh Chari's *Don't wait, make things happen* is one such book that doesn't sermonize, but goads you to get down to brass tacks then and there.

Before descanting upon Dr Chari's superb book, it's imperative to know his credentials and antecedents. Dr Suresh Chari is a well-known corporate and soft skills trainer and motivator who has been motivating and galvanizing professionals for more than four decades. He has profound knowledge of all the facets integral to his training programs and is focused on his objective. In corporate parlance, we can say that Suresh Chari knows his onions.

Therefore, this book is what we call in Sanskrit, *Sanchitgyaankosham* (accumulated and encapsulated repertoire of wisdom). Most importantly, he understands the psychology of those he deals with and guides. He has penned this book to guide and motivate youth. Nowhere in the book does he sound didactic or pontificating. Flaunting his knowledge and vast experience is not the goal, but serving young professionals to achieve what they aspire to is Chari's cardinal aim.

The moment you hold the book in your hands, you feel as if you're being personally guided. In this book, he has summarised his friendly teaching in 12 attributes: Attitude, Adaptability, Awareness, Ambition, and Accountability, among others. One may say that others have also touched upon these aspects. Indeed, they've written on these points before. But, Chari has written with first-hand experience of varied and myriad situations, people and their practical problems. The pragmatism of his case studies, behavioural patterns and habits mentioned in the book will grab the attention of the readers. They'll be motivated to implement the mantras of success the author has formulated for them.

The relatability quotient of his practical examples is something that must be lauded and to me, this is the USP of Suresh Chari's immensely readable book. To cut the matter short, *Don't wait, make things happen* **has the wherewithal to provide fodder to youth and professionals, belonging to all fields and spheres. So, don›t wait. Pick up a copy of it! All the best.**

– SUMIT PAUL, a Poona-based advanced research scholar of Semitic Civilizations, Cultures and Languages

Gratitude

This book is a synergy of the thoughts of all the participants of my Personal Growth Training sessions spread over more than the past four decades. My gratitude to all these students, teachers, parents, family, professionals, executives, entrepreneurs, members of social organizations and friends who have knowingly or unknowingly contributed to the content of this book.

My gratitude to Dr Ved Prakash Mishra, a powerful orator and an illustrious intellect who promoted me in various training platforms from my school days. I am fortunate to have such a versatile, multitalented, multi-tasker and able administrator as my friend, philosopher and mentor all through my life. I am thankful that such a high-profile, busy academician went through the draft copy critically and wrote the forward.

My thanks are due to Mr Sumit Paul for writing the second forward for this book. He is an advanced research scholar of Semitic Civilizations, Cultures and Languages and is a freelance contributor to the world's premier publications in multiple languages. His books have always inspired millions of readers and I am no exception. I am happy such a versatile writer could find time to read and appreciate this book.

I am grateful to Mr Murli Chari, my school mate, friend and accomplished writer for accepting to edit the manuscript. His command and flow of the English language are beyond compare. During the pandemic, we all went online and Murli could attend my training sessions and that was when he suggested, "Suresh, why don't you write about what you say in your training programmes on personal growth?" His pursuance resulted in the scripting of this book. He also volunteered to add a few appropriate anecdotes.

I wish to place my deep sense of gratitude to Junior Chamber International (JCI), an individual development organization that fostered my personal growth as a trainer and provided me with a platform to experiment with my thoughts and transform them into personal growth sessions. There were several stalwart trainers whom I met during my association with JCI and who have been a source of inspiration for me to go on with my training.

I must thank my dear colleagues at the workplace, especially Dr Madhur, Dr Shubhada, Dr Anne, Dr Debashish and Dr Saee for always being there for me at the right place and at the right time. They have been a true critic of my training inputs. Thanks are due to my friend Mr Ajay Raibole, Adjunct Faculty, Government College of Arts and Design for the creative illustrations.

My special thanks to my friend Dr Rupali a school principal, soft skills trainer and an English language teacher who has very critically analysed the contents as a common reader.

Thanks to my family, my wife Kalpana, a former school teacher, my son Dr Rahul and my daughter-in-law Dr Rucha, both dentists, for their magnificent support and contribution to my journey.

I wish to dedicate this book to the memory of two great men in my life who have positively influenced me; my father Late Shri C.N. Chari and my PhD guide Late Dr Nirmal Nath.

Don't Wait, Make Things Happen

The twelve attributes of an effective personality

Dr Suresh Chari

Preface

I regularly conduct Personality, Communication and Leadership Enrichment Training Programmes for all age groups after which on many occasions several of my participants demanded a book to be written on these issues that they could refer to later. The idea sounded good but I kept telling them that conducting a training program is my forte, not writing. Speaking, convincing and attempting to make people think differently in my programs is a unique experience and I think I am good at it, but authoring a book is another domain which I had not explored.

However, there was something else in store where close friends and mentors motivated me and said, "Keep writing as if you are speaking". And that's how this book came into existence. That's the reason in many places you will feel I am conversing with you rather than writing. I am told that my training programmes are highly rated, only because they are user friendly. That is, people can relate to the common household examples and simplicity of language. In all these training programmes, there is normally a mix of simple English and Hindi without jargon. I have tried to keep this reputation intact in this book and all through you will find examples commonly occurring in your house, workplace or society and a language that can be understood easily by all.

The title of the book *Don't wait, make things happen* relates to my firm belief that each one of us can create our own destiny and hence we need to allow destiny to take charge of our lives but design our own life: make things happen. I also believe that this can happen at any stage of life for anyone.

This book is not meant to be a *pravachan* (discourse).

It is an essence of my experience of life. It is a compilation of my experience of life. This book is the offshoot of several training programmes conducted by me with thousands of participants. As the saying goes 'teaching is learning twice'.

It has been more than four decades since I have been conducting these programmes. As my participants learnt and enriched themselves, so did I creating a win-win situation for the trainer and the trainee.

My sessions have always been very interactive, where there was a free flow of ideas, sharing of experiences, etc. This two-way traffic of interactive sessions helped me learn in the process, bettering it day by day and session after session. Moreover, my training programmes are comprehensive as they include a diverse population of varied ages and gender. Participants from varied age groups and backgrounds (social, economical, educational,etc.) are a part of it. This strengthened my erudition and fortified my conviction to share with you the 'twelve' attributes that could help you look at life differently and more positively.

Read this book not because something is terribly wrong with us but because we all are good and want to become better. We are also at the same time free to choose our ways of life and disagree with me. There are a few essentials in life that, if adopted, can phenomenally enhance the quality of our life. These 12 attributes are prerequisites to "make things happen," which if implemented would skyrocket our life to one of purpose and meaning.

These 'twelve' attributes will make things happen for you.

The philosophy of 'make things happen' hinges on the 12 attributes. These attributes are extremely vital as they would provide strategic direction for leading a fulfilling life. A meticulous imbibing of the 12 attributes will vouch for a life full of happiness and harmony. It does not guarantee a problem-free life but surely does endure to platter us with solutions for these problems.

These 12 attributes are independent yet interwoven. These cannot be learnt and practised in isolation as one attribute supports another.

We have to practice these 12 attributes so much that they should get into our blood, under our skin thus becoming our second nature.

A religious effort in this direction will help us to inculcate these attributes. If we connect these dots of the 12 attributes, we definitely create a BIG picture of ourselves.

The 12 attributes required to 'make things happen' and that I am going to elaborate on are here for our reference.

1. Attitude and Perception

2. Adaptability

3. Awareness about self

4. Ambitious with clear goals

5. Accountable

6. Acceptable and Approachable

7. Apart:Being creative and innovative

8. Ambivert's ability to choose between behaviours of extrovert and introvert

9. Active speaker

10. Assertive communication with rationality and empathy

11. Appreciation

12. Do you have a feedback partner?

God give us the strength...

Let me start with a three-line prayer that I follow regularly.

This prayer, written by Reinhold Niebuhr, has given me immense solace and is an almost stress-free life (almost, because it is difficult to imagine life without minimum stress).

Line 1: ***God, give me the serenity to accept the things that I cannot change.***

Line 2: ***God, give me the courage to change the things I can.***

Line 3: ***God, give me the wisdom to know the difference between the two.***

When we ponder over this prayer, we realise that we often come across such people or situations in life. Many a time, it is difficult to face such situations in our close-knit family and extended families.

There are many people or situations in life that we cannot change.

I lost my father in 2008 and my mother is now 92 years and, like all 90-plus, she behaves and speaks like a five-year-old. She goes back to her childhood. She has numerous questions and does not hesitate to ask them without bothering about thetiming or who is around.

Where are you going? When will you come back? Are you going to be late today also? These are simple questions and can be dealt with but when she starts making emotional statements like,"Nobody wants to talk to me.No one spends time with me nowadays. I am now alone in life. You all are waiting for me to die.Why don't you people inform me earlier when you are eating out.So much food is wasted daily,"etc., etc.

When these questions/statements are fired at us on a regular daily and hourly basis, then they start testing our patience and that is the time I remember the first and second lines of the prayer. I cannot change my mother! I cannot change or stop her questions. I cannot lose my patience with her statements that I think are sometimes irritating, hence I pray,"God, give me the strength to accept my mother as she is" (line 1) and "God, give me the courage to use different methods to deal with her so that I do not lose my cool" (line 2).

I know all 92 years old mothers are not like this but there are many such people or situations at home, workplace and society where if we cannot change the person or situation, then we can change ourselves or change the way we deal with that person or situation.

I understand that this is easier said than done. Some people or situations are very difficult and extremely rigid. In fact, difficult people create difficult situations. Man being a social animal, cannot live in isolation. Therefore, dealing with such people becomes inevitable.

But do we really have a choice? These people may be very close to us or in our inner circle and we do not wish to lose them. Moreover, in the first line of the prayer to God, we have sought for the 'strength to accept them' since we cannot and should not attempt to change them. What is in our hands is the second line—the 'courage to change the things we can'. 'Courage', because to accept to change ourselves or our methods needs us to keep our 'ego' out.

It's quite possible that we have not tried enough to change our methods with such *difficult* people or situations. My experience advocates that we keep trying different ways of handling such people and situations. Now sit back relax and think if we have taken efforts with such people whom we cannot change yet do not want to lose.

Of course, the last line of the prayer is the most important. We need to have the wisdom to know who or what can be changed and what cannot be. We cannot make amistake here.

This book follows these three lines especially the second one: "God give me the courage to change the things I can". One thing that is in our hands is changing 'ourselves', our approach towards people and situations. We cannot change the basic nature of people but we can make them think differently.

Yesterday I was clever, so I wanted to change the world; today I am wise so I am changing myself.

Let us begin with the first attribute which is the foundation for the rest of the virtues.

1

Attitude and Perception:

The First Attribute to make Things Happen

The way you think is the way you act

We need to understand the difference between the above two words. In simple words, perception is the way we think and attitude is the action (behaviour) happening out of the way we think. So, perception comes first followed by action. I strongly believe that the way we think decides the way we act. Thinking decides the action. If I put it the other way around; look at our action (attitude or behaviour) others understand how we think or our action tells us about our thought process.

We cannot expect to get oranges while sitting under a mango tree. If we think negative our actions will be negative. If we think positive, our actions will be positive. When we are in a conversation with people athome, workplace or in society, people only look at our behaviour or action and come to conclusions about how we must be thinking. Hence, our ***behaviour reflects our personality.***

This could be unfortunate, but people do judge us by our behaviour and form opinions about us. So, it's important to check our behaviour in situations where we are surrounded by people who form opinions about us like in workplace meetings, first encounters, parties, social gatherings, family get-togethers, interviews, group discussions, etc.

It is important to care for what people think about us provided they are our inner circle people or feedback partners. However, what we think of ourselves is more important than what others think of us. Low self-esteem breeds an inferiority complex. We thus allow people around to define us as weak, or bad.

Our behaviour reflects how we think about ourselves, others or situations. If we think we are no good, bad, weak, small, etc., we will act similarly. On the contrary, if we think we are good or like the other person or the situation our actions with ourselves or with the person or with the situation will be positive.

So, the first attribute is to ***think positive*** so that our attitude (action) will be reflected as positive. ***This is challenging since I am advocating that we think positive despite all the negativities around us.*** Although it may sound difficult in all situations, believe me with practice this is possible.

There is a famous adage "A man with a single arm with a positive attitude can beat anytime a man with both arms with a negative attitude". To emphasise the importance of attitude further the saying "Our attitude decides our altitude" is apt. Best of talents sans attitude is of no avail. A burst tyre and a bad attitude will not allow you to move further unless changed. A bad attitude is ubiquitous and that is one of the reasons forfailures.

Let's look at a few iconic personalities with positive perceptions who have evoked "Wow what an attitude!" from us. One classic example of great attitude is that of legendary Dr Helen Keller who despite myriad afflictions did a marvellous job and is an inspirational example for all of us who are endowed with so many skills and talents yet still crib and whine.

A positive attitude enables us to foray into a near-impossible assignment despite so many constraints. Japan which was devastated rose like a Phoenix from the ashes of World War II and became a renowned developed economy. Our own legendary Ravindra Jain was a great musician, lyricist, and singer par excellence despite his being blind. To understand the enormity of attitude it is recommended to read *Attitude is Everything* by Jeff Keller.

If we want to make things happen we need to have a positive perception despite all odds that shall be reflected in our attitude or action. If we give due importance and credence to attitude, our lives will grow by leaps and bounds.

2

Adaptability

The Second Attribute to make Things Happen

Closely Associated with the Words Change and Comfort Zone

Move out of your comfort zone

We need to tweak Charles Darwin's famous quote "Survival of the fittest' to "Survival of the most adaptable". Human beings have evolved over many millennia through this singular virtue whereas the mighty dinosaurs have become extinct. Even humble cockroaches have adapted beautifully to survive for millions of years. It has been observed, rightly so, those who adapt flourish and those who do not, perish. We need to embrace change and adopt new technologies, cultures, and practices.

I remember my school biology teachers telling me two simple yet wonderful examples of adaptability. One that of blades of grass stands the storm and gets back to its original stature. The second is water which takes its course despite all impediments.

This has been beautifully explained by Dr Spencer Johnson in his extremely popular book *Who moved my cheese?*Many people are left in the lurch as they fail to adapt. Dr Alvin Toffler in his epoch book *Future Shock* has portrayed the rapid changes which put many people in a quandary.

Kodak who was the market leader in marketing camera rolls and traditional cameras failed to read the writing on the wall. Even Nokia who was indubitably the Numero Uno in mobiles was left behind. So, adaptability is a vital skill to flourish.

During the current pandemic those who embraced technology progressed by leaps and bounds. Many traditional businesses will be dead as a dodo if they fail to resort to the most important skill of adaptability. We would have been still living in the caves had we not adapted to the new environs. With the speed at which things are changing, this vital skill would be the game changer.

Pramod Batra in his book *Management Thoughts*says, "Human mind is like a parachute; it works only when it is open". In all my training sessions I ask the participants to try and work out why Dr Batra must have used this analogue of comparing a human mind with a parachute. Some say the mind should be as free to go up as a parachute, while few say mind and parachute both go high up to work, etc. After much deliberation, they emerge with this statement, "Sir, what is the use of a parachute that does not open at the right time." And that's what I think Dr Batra intended to say. What is the use of a mind that does not open at the right time? When we are attending a seminar or reading a book like this and if our mind is closed how can we absorb anything?

Our mind should be like a sponge, ready to absorb. The mind should also be like a strainer holding back what is good for oneself and letting go of what is bad.

Keeping an open mind is nothing but being adaptable whichis the ability to listen to others' point of view. We may not agree withothers but at least listen! On the contrary, rigid people have shut themselves down from others' views and actually stopped their growth in the process. There was a time maybe during our father's or grandfather's time when people were rigid and yet successful. But not anymore.

Change is the only constant. It is a natural process and will happen by default and we cannot stop change from happening. It is inevitable. It is because of adapting to change that mankind has progressed overthese years.

However, in the 21st century, the quantum and the speed of change have increased multifold. More so in India. Name any field—science, technology, health science, education, fashion, cinema, environmental science, engineering, sports, infrastructure, or politics—it is evident everywhere. If one has to cope with this increasing size and pace of change then one has to be adaptable or flexible an important attribute to make things happen.

I have been a medical teacher for44 years and have survived the process successfully only because I have been able to alter my teaching methods in accordance with the changing needs of the student in the class.

Life is meant for forward progression. As stagnant water gets contaminated, a stagnant life may become drudgery. We get halted and get into the routine and mundane rut of things as we are not ready to switch gears to make our life better. The biggest hurdle in this context is the trap of our own **comfort zone**.

Comfort zones are areas where we feel comfortable operating. There is nothing wrong withworking from our comfort zone. However, some comfort zones are also habits which we do not want to shed and we are aware that if we move out of these habits, we can be more successful but we do not, because they are our comfort zones. Once we identify these habits that are stopping us from progressing and move away from them, we can experience phenomenal growth.

Let me give you some typical examples of such habits: getting up late, laziness, procrastination, emotional attachments, friends, mobile, social media, negative thinking, blaming situations and we can add many more. Some are useful and good. But if any one of these habits is coming between us and our success and we are not able to shed them away then these comfort zones become dangerous.

Apart from habits, one big culprit that stops us from progressing is when were main in our comfort zone of 'fear of failure' and would not like to venture into newer areas.

If we do not come out of our comfort zones we will be thrown out and will not be able to catch up with the pace of the changing times.

Comfort zones are sometimes also 'mindsets' or things we have been traditionally following often blindly. One of the main reasons to develop such a frame of mind is the paucity of knowledge.Here if we are talking aboutcoping with change, then I am of the firm belief that not all traditions need to be followed in 2022.

One such mindset is about the division of work as 'men's work' and 'ladies' work'. In India, this is more visible. Women are meant for household work; look after children and other members at home while men are bread earners. Much has changed and its time these mindsets also change and people move out of these comfort zones. I am very happy that the present generation of parents isrealising this and we can see many parents sharing all the chores at home without gender bias especially when both parents are working.

I stay in a community apartment where about 18 families live in different flats and every morning I witness both parents rushing their children with school bags in hand to see them off at the bus stop or school van or an autorickshaw. I have also seen both parents attending the parent-teacher meetings and social gathering events of their child in the school. This is a very positive sign. I do not remember my father ever doing this! Even if it is done out of compulsion the child at home who learns mostly by seeing is being educated to realise that there is no such thing as 'men's work' and 'ladies' work'. In fact, the frightful pandemic has never less given us a lesson on delegation of work at home and how to move out of our comfort zones or 'mindsets'.

Let me give you a frightful example. I have a very dear friend who has always seen the tradition of 'men's work' and 'ladies' work' being followed ritually at his home. He was fortunate to get married to a woman who did all the household chores religiously and sincerely. They have two children, both boys and the tradition continued. All men would sit at the dining table and expect hot *rotis* (Indian bread) while the lady of the house-baked it for them continuously. After the meal, all three men would rest while the lady was still busy cleaning up the utensils, mopping the floor and doing all the other odd jobs including preparing for the next meal. Children learn by watching their parents and these two boys learnt that there is something called 'men's work' and 'ladies work' and that is the way of life. Things were fine till the elder son got married and who remained still in his comfort zone or mindset of 'men's work' and 'ladies' work'. The young lady, the daughter-in-law of the house was a working woman and in her house, she had always seen men and women working together. Sadly, the marriage lasted only for one year.

Hence, it is essential that we move out of our comfort zones if not for ourselves but for thegeneration next.

All great people have achieved great heights only when they have moved out of their comfort zones. Read the life stories of successful people we admire, they may be Sachin Tendulkar, Dhirubhai Ambani, Shah Rukh Khan, or any one we idolise from any field. Read closely about their growth stories and we will find that they all moved out of their comfort zones to reach the pinnacle of success.

We can also draw inspiration from our family members, relatives and friends by observing their good habits and trying to imbibe them into our lifestyle. The challenging task is first to have the wisdom to accept that such habits or comfort zones are responsible for slowing the pace of one's success. Once identified, we should have the courage to move out of these comfort zones.

If we want to make things happen then we need to try and connect the words. Open Mind-Adaptability-Change-Comfort Zone

1. Only people who keep their minds open can demonstrate adaptability or flexibility.

2. If we want to cope with the speed and size of the change, we have to be adaptable.

3. Finally, only such people can demonstrate the above, if they have the ability to identify habits that block their growth and move out of their comfort zones.

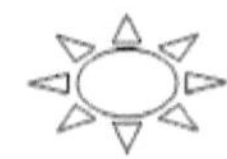

3

Awareness

Third Attribute to make Things Happen

Awareness about Self: The Magic of SWOT Analysis

Awareness about Situations and People Around

The Magic of SWOT

Most of us are zombies going through regimented and robotic motions. Being aware of oneself makes us take conscious decisions and actions. Awareness is about being fully grounded in the present. Once we are aware of ourselves, we are in full control of the situation. Once we live with full awareness, we attract immense affluence.

Self-Image

"A package of beliefs that we carry around in our head, that we have accepted to be true about ourselves whether it is true or not".

Self-image is the mental picture of how we see our self. No one is born with a low or high self-image. It is defined and shaped at an early age. How people around us have been treating us during our early years of infancy to childhood? Family and friends can contribute to a poor self-image. If we have been receiving negative strokes like "You are useless" "Can't you do this much?" "You are not good at anything" "Look how he/she is better than you in talking, music, behaviour, studies, etc., etc." then we are bound to be more influenced by negative self-image and will slowly develop a low self-image of our self with "I am no good" written all around us.

The good news is that we have the power to change our self-image which can boost our self-confidence. Our inside appearance is more important than our outward appearance. More importantly, once we learn to love and accept our self, our outward appearance and experiences will emulate the way we feel inside. Remember, it's all in our heads!

One of the ways of enhancing self-image and hence self-confidence is by the magic of *self-talk*. This involves talking to ourselves about our strengths and reassuring our self with statements like "I am good" and "I can do it".Even a simple statement like "let me try" can work wonders for our confidence.

We must pay regular visits to own selves. A SWOT analysis is where we list down our (S) Strengths, (W) Weaknesses (O) Create opportunities to convert our weaknesses into our strengths and work on the (T) Threats that accompany them. We may need the help of a close associate to get true feedback on SWOT.

It's just amazing to notice that each one of us has many strengths which we have never looked at as strengths and very few weaknesses.

The wonderful thing is once we realise that this is our weakness we have won half the battle with that weakness. How can we remove something that we cannot see? My father was an angry young man, an angry middle age man and died an angry old man. My friends were scared to visit my house if 'Tiger' (my father) was at home. I told my father several times, "Dad, why do you get so angry and shout at people? My friends do not come home because of this nature of yours." Do you know what was the reply I got? "Who, says I get angry? No, I never get angry."

The moral of the story is that my father could never see that anger comes between him and his relationships. He could never realise that anger is his weakness. He would have been able to do away with this emotion had he seen or realised that anger is a problem! So, we can remove only those things that we can see as our weaknesses. I repeat: if we have seen or put on paper our weaknesses we have won half the battle. So, converting your weakness to strength involves three steps:(i) see it or realise that it's a weakness; (ii)accept it, and (iii) do something about it (Take action. Create an opportunity to minimise the weakness).

Not surprisingly one of the most common weaknesses listed by my participants in several programmes is 'anger'. Yes, it's a weakness when anger comes between us and our relationships. It's not wrong to get and express this emotion called anger. It's understandable to get angry once in a while. However, it's detrimental if it happens too very often and is often repeated as a behaviour. I strongly believe that a constantly repeated behaviour is a habit and at the drop of the hat this emotion of anger is expressed as a habit. I know it's tough to control or manage anger. But conscious and consistent efforts to realise the harmful effects of anger will make us look for methods of minimising anger if not completely doing away with it.

It needs the courage of conviction to accept the fact that we have been angry with a person when it was not necessary. When we see anger coming we have that split second or a moment to see it coming or we can realise that we are about to get angry. We can feel the adrenaline rush. That's the moment in our hands. Decide not to get angry. Use several techniques, such as, time-out (postponement), drinking a glass of water, reverse counting, staying quiet and trying to internally calm our self.

Let's take one more common example of weaknesses. "Sir, I am not able to speak confidently in front of a small crowd." The opportunities are using platforms to start with short speeches like a vote of thanks, the introduction of speakers, etc. These opportunities have to be created. Take small steps, to begin with. They will be accompanied bythreats like fear of ridicule, failure, comparison, etc. which are mostly self-created and it's all 'in our heads'. Ignore these threats, use the opportunities several times and slowly but surely this weakness of "not being able to speak in front of a gathering" will go away and it can be listed as our strength.

Hence seeing it as a weakness, accepting and action with 'positive self-talk' are the medicines to convert your weakness into strength, to convert low self-image to high self-image and low self-confidence to high self-confidence.

Answer this Questionnaire

Remember: the first answer that comes to your mind is the best

Tick one option:

- Most people like me   always/sometimes/never/can't say

- I enjoy my work   always/sometimes/never/can't say

- I am an interesting person   always/sometimes/never/can't say

- I am comfortable during conversationsalways/sometimes/never/can't say

- Nothing is too good for me   always/sometimes/never/can't say

- I like where I live   always/sometimes/never/can't say

- I like my looks/appearance   always/sometimes/never/can't say

- I am satisfied with myself   always/sometimes/never/can't say

- I am an optimistic person   always/sometimes/never/can't say

- Other people care about me   always/sometimes/never/can't say

- I feel I am a kind person   always/sometimes/never/can't say

- People value my opinion   always/sometimes/never/can't say

- I am in a good mood   always/sometimes/never/can't say

  **You have just died; your photo is placed and your friends want to write about you "Here was a person who ....

  ....

  ....(Complete the sentence in 15-20 words)

If you have finished the above questionnaire, then read on…

We may have ticked "sometimes" for many statements. That's okay.

I will just take one example. "Most people like me" if we have ticked sometimes, then we know sometimes people do not like us. Identify that as our weakness and try to find out when are the times or what are the issues that people do not like us or about us. We may not get the ideal "Always" answer for all the statements but we will try to reach there. But a "Never" or "Don't know" are avoidable issues.

Why did I make you write the double-starred statement: you have just died?

This is how we would like to be remembered after our death. And hence, we shall have to live like that from today itself. Each word that we have written in this statement is important and must be emulated or expressed from now onwards.

Worksheet 2

Write quietly on a piece of paper

1. Two habits you want to change that come between you and success

2. What do people like about you?

3. What do people criticise you about?

4. What are the things that you wish to change in yourself in the near future?

5. What would you like to be remembered for?

I strongly recommend that we cross-check the information with our close feedback partners or inner-circle people.

Do they feel the same about us?

Do they concur with our answers?

This is our complete SWOT analysis. Today, big corporates and successful companies are constantly encouraging their employees to do their SWOT and also actively engage in doing their company's SWOT analysis.

If we want to make things happen then we need to be constantly engaged in SWOT analysis to be more successful in life.

4

Ambitious with Clear Goals

Fourth Attribute to make Things Happen

An aimless life is a useless life

My uncle who was a Swamiji with Ramakrishna Ashram told me this story when I was in 11thstandard. Two donkeys were very good friends. One was a *dhobi's* donkey (washerman) and another one was a *madari's* donkey (one who goes from street to street making young children walk on a rope. Tightrope walking). Dhobhi's donkey used to always tell the Madari's donkey, "Your job has so much work, going from one street to another carrying the material and yourdaughter, the tight rope walker. Look at my job; one trip in the morning with dirty clothes to the lake. Then take rest the whole day. Then one more trip back home in the evening. That's all. Why don't you join my owner's company? I will recommend your name to my boss. He will definitely take you."

But the Madari's donkey would always say, "I am happy where I am, leave me alone." Finally, the Dhobhi's donkey curiously asked the Madari's donkey, "What is it that excites you there? Why do you still keep working for the stupid job even when you know it's thankless?"And this is what the Madari's donkey had to say, "When the daughter of the Madari is walking on the rope, the Madari always tells the daughter, 'walk properly.If you fall, I will get you married to this donkey'. And I am waiting for that day when the daughter will fall and then I will get married to her."

I looked at my uncle and smiled. He said, "Smile you may but do you have the courage to listen to the moral of the story?" I said, "Yes, tell me."Swamiji said, "Look, Suresh, even a donkey has an aim…and you are a human being." He said, "An aimless life is a useless life; how can you travel when you do not know where you want to go? Have you ever played a game of football or soccer without a goal post?" That's when I became serious about what I need to do in my life in future. Although, let me confess I still was not clear as to what I would do ahead but the story kept reminding me that I need to set a goal for myself. I need to know what I have to do. How I would look at myself five years from now. If I know about my destination and what is in store for me, life becomes all the more exciting.

If we are told we are to go for a picnic tomorrow morning at six am with our dear friends, how do we feel the previous night? Excited! The same is with life. If we know there is something to look forward to, the days ahead become exciting and we are charged to do all that it takes to reach there.

Being ambitious is good. Dreaming is good. I am reminded of Dr Abdul Kalam who once said, "Dream is not that which you see while sleeping, it is something that does not let you sleep."

Ray Kroc was very clear about his ambitious goal to have outlets of McDonald's across the globe when he had only a $20 bill. Dhirubhai Ambani dreamt of starting an oil company when he was born into a very poor family. The legendary president of America Abraham Lincoln was very clear on what he wanted for his country. In the absence of clarity, we just move around like leaves in the air.

Excellence is never an accident; it is the result of high intention, sincere efforts, intelligent direction, skilful execution and the vision to see obstacles as opportunities.

I am also reminded of these four lines in Hindi, "*Kaun kehta hai ki haatoo ki lakir takdeer banati hai. Takdeer tu unke bhi hote jinke haat nahi hote*" (Who says the lines on our palms define our destiny, even people without hands have a destiny"). It means that though there are destiny lines on our hands, we can still create our own destiny if we follow these five steps:

1. Set clear goals—first long-term goals and then break them down into short-term goals

2. Focus on the short-term goals without losing sight of the long-term goal

3. Identify and then minimise distractions

4. Micro plan schedules and

5. Act upon them

In all my programmes on 'Goal Setting,' I allow my participants to ponder over seven magic words of goal setting.

1. Challenging

2. Achievable

3. Specific

4. Dated

5. Written

6. Reviewable with a reference group

7. Burning desire

Have you ever been to an exhibition or a fair? There is a stall of Ring Toss, where the stall owner will give you three rings to throw at articles placed at a reasonable distance in four rows. The first row of articles is generally the low-priced ones like some cheap soaps or toothpaste, etc. The second row is relatively more expensive and the final two rows are fairly expensive. Where do we throw our first ring? Generally, we try for the first or the second row and we hit the target or ringer as it is called. Where do we target our second ring? Think carefully, it's generally the third-row articles or if we are sure about our self, the fourth row. I am tempted to compare this activity with life goals. Yes, goals should be challenging like aiming for the fourth row with the most expensive articles but they should be achievable.

Challenging and achievable are two wonderful words. They are very subjective and will differ from person to person. Hence, I will never advise anyone to compare goals witheach other because the achievability factors differ from person to person. Yes, but goals SHOULD BE challenging. What is challenging? A little more than what we can achieve.

What is included in achievability factors? Our capacity to work hard, dedication, sincerity, ability to keep distractions away, ability to move out of our comfort zone (Chapter 1) and ability to identify our weaknesses and the courage to convert them into strengths (Chapter 3), ability to identify those habits or characteristics or issues that we fall short of to reach to that challenging goal that we have set for ourselves. It may also include our financial situation, and motivating or de-motivating factors at home or in our inner circle.

Let me give you an example. We set our goal asclearing theentrance examination forIAS. Is it challenging? Yes. What will be the answer tothe question?Is it achievable? Do we have many abilities like the ones mentioned above? Will we be able to tackle or get over our weaknesses or disabling factors? If the answer is yes, then we look for IAS as a challenging target and start preparing for the same keeping in mind all the achievable factors required to reach our goal.

Let's have a look at another common example. "Sir, I want to get into engineering then MBA or become a doctor, lawyer, architect, fashion designer, writer, artist" or so many other options that India is offering today. All these goals could become challenging if we look at the third magic word and be more **specific**. Engineering or any career from the best university followed by MBA or post-graduation from an A+ institute. Now sit back and think of the achievability factors that we possess,i.e., our strengths and weaknesses to reach there. Use our strengths and take action to convert the weaknesses into strengths.

I asked one of my participants, "All this is fine, your career goals are challenging yet achievable and are specific, but when would you be able to reach there?" He said, "Someday,sir.One day you will be proud of your student." This is meaningless. A goal without a date or timeline will never be a reality.

Let's take an example. If we are 16 today in 2022 and have targeted to become a doctor, graduating and post-graduating from AIIMS and proceeding to do cardiology from PGI Chandigarh, then all this has to be **dated** (the fourth magic word). Each milestone has to be a year marked on the paper that we are using to write our goals. 2027 MBBS, 2030 post-graduation in medicine and 2033 super speciality in cardiology. This will keep reminding us of what we need to do in the next six months and the year ahead. The long-term goal of becoming a cardiologist needs to be broken down into small or short-term six months' goals with dates and challenges that may be encountered while achieving them. The same logic and process are true with any career we want to pursue.

It's not that this process of goal setting applies only to students. It is not related to age or gender. If one is ambitious, then growth is an ongoing process. Someone rightly said,"You are never too old to dream a new dream". As an adult, several times we wish to think of growth midway through our careers either in the same organization where we are employed or in business or as an entrepreneur or as a homemaker.

This is necessary because one should keep moving ahead in life. Moreover, don't we get bored with the mundane routine of the job we are doing day in and day out? Hence setting fresh targets can happen anytime in life to anyone. But only thinking of growth at this stage of life will not help. We have to visualise, plan and organise our short-term goals to reach the long-term goal. They all must be dated. Unless there is a timeline for each step, the short and eventually long-term goals will not be reached.

The draft proforma below could be useful in **writing** (sixth magic word) down our six-month plans. A written goal document is important to keep reminding us of the goal we have set for our self and the challenges therein. When we write the goal, we are committed to it. Moreover, at times when we feel low or dejected or may feel it's not feasible, that's the time we look at this written sheet and get charged all over again.

A word of caution, though. This is one such document that I would never recommend anyone to share with any Tom-Dick-Harry. It is a very personal and sensitive document. If it falls in the wrong hands, then we may be subjected to negative comments or mockery about our set goals, which hurts very badly and could affect our life goal plans. I would recommend that we share them with our inner circle or 'Reference group' as I call them; people who will guide us to rethink or re-organise the dates and sometimes even suggest slightly altering our goals since they know our strengths and weaknesses.

That's where the fifth magic word pops up which is **reviewable**. At the same time, I do not advocate too much of changes in the goal plan lest it dilutes our efforts. But there are times in life when certain inevitable or unavoidable things happen thatwe had never foreseen when we sat down to structure our goals. This is when minor reviews are recommended. That's when our inner circle or reference group comes to our rescue. These are people who are our true feedback partners and caring well-wishers. They may be your father, mother, brother, sister, relative, friend or teacher. They know us well enough to influence us and our goals and suggest a few alterations in plans depending on the present situation that necessitates these alterations. The pleasure of celebration after the attainment of the goals ismultifold or greater when we achieve and celebrate them alongside our inner circle.

The eighth word **Burning Desire** is in my opinion the most important word. How will we feel if we attain the goal or fail to do so? There has to be an inner strong desire to accomplish and complete the set goals, and then we would work on our goals in any circumstance, adverse or good.

I would recommend that we read the book titled *The Secret* by Rhonda Byrne whichtalks of the law of attraction the essence of the book is if we have a strong desire to achieve something eventually we shall reach there. *When we strongly think of things we want, and we focus with all our intention, then the law of attraction will give us exactly what we want, every time.* Such is the power of having a burning desire to achieve something.

So, the secret is to BE FOCUSED. Being focused does not necessarily mean we cannot have some fun, dance, sing or party. It does not mean we cannot enjoy life. What it means is we are selfish towards our goal but we know when, where, how much and with whom to enjoy. This is one place where *selfish* is not a dirty word. There is nothing wrong withbeing 'selfish' towards our goal. It is in this context that the word *selfish* has been used here. And when we are selfish, we are focused, we are not distracted, and we keep away from distracting elements including things and people.

If we want to make things happen then we need to spend time with people who are with our goal-setting programme, who do not discourage us and who push us towards our goal at times when the focus is flickering. So, the secret is to BE FOCUSED.

My written Goal Proforma

1. My name:.............

2. My long-term goal:..........

3. Specific goal I wish to achieve in the next six months:......

4. This goal is important to me because..............

5. If I attain it, I will feel:..............

6. If I do not attain it, I will feel:..............

7. The obstacles are: People:...................

    Things:..................

8. I plan to overcome these obstacles by:...........

9. My resources and support system in accomplishing my goals

    People:............

    Things: ....

10. I intend to use these helps by:.........

11. The specific steps I intend to take to reach my goals are:

a. Steps:...........

b. I will begin by:............

c. My target date to finish is: ....

Signature

5

Accountable

Fifth Attribute to make Things Happen

Taking Responsibility, Being Disciplined and Time Conscious

Taking responsibility, being disciplined and time consious

Accountability is when we take responsibility for our own actions. I am Suresh and I have a twin brother named Ramesh. I still remember during our childhood, if my father had to post a letter he would give it to Ramesh because he was sure that at the end of the day Ramesh would post that letter and if given to me the same would still remain in my upper shirt pocket. That's when I learnt the meaning of accountability. Such a simple example had such a profound impact on me about taking responsibility and being responsible. Ever since then I have tried to attach that label behind my back that "Suresh is a *responsible* person, *dependable* and *trustworthy*". See how beautifully these three words are interwoven.

Today I am proud to say that whatever role I have played as a son, student, friend, teacher, husband, father and now grandfather, these words have given me that extra edge to grow and be acceptable amidst others. People look at me with respect. Yes, if we are accountable, respect automatically follows. "Once given a task to Suresh, be rest assured that it will be accomplished" that's how people around me speak about me. This attribute has always placed me above the rest. That's what differentiates an ordinary from anextraordinary person.

Being accountable is an outcome of being disciplined in life. It's a virtue, a value that one can cherish all through our life. Persons who are disciplined do not need external motivation for every task that they undertake. They are self-motivated. They are self-starters. They are proactive and believe that"Don't wait for things to happen, make things happen".

When Kinetic Honda launched its first moped, ithad a tag line. "You don't have to kick me anymore; I have a self-starter". Simple tasks like "I don't need my mother to wake me up in the morning to study, since I have my alarm clock. I don't need to be pushed by my parents to keep reminding me constantly 'go and study', I do it myself". Believe me, all your parental pressures of "Do this or do that" will vanish once they know that you are a self-starter, accountable or responsible.

Two names strike our mind when we speak of discipline: one is that of legendary Kapil Dev the great all-rounder cricketer who never missed out on a match due to injury as he kept his physical fitness in great shape and the second is Amitabh Bachchan who even though nearing 80 is fit as a fiddle as he takes responsibility of all the facets of his life.

We should take charge of our lives. We should be in the driver's seat so that we can steer our life in the right direction. Moreover, all the other controls also remain in our hands. They help us either to stop or slow down or accelerate our speed (of life) as circumstances warrant.

Time conscious: The easiest way to insult a person is by not valuing his or her time. Being late with genuine reasons once in a while is okay. But being **always** late is not acceptable since it can become a habit. There could be two reasons. One is that we are not well organised and the second more dangerous one is we like to make people wait for us!

Time management has a new title now and it's called 'Priority Management'. If we are not organised, it means that we are not able to prioritise our daily activities as per our schedule into three categories namely,most important, not so important and avoidable activities. If there is an exam looming ahead or a target to be completed in our organization, I am sure a focused person will set priorities and schedule the daily routine accordingly and keep the distractions or recreational activities away or to a minimum for a while till the exams or task is over.

However, if we like to make people wait for us, then we are actually demonstrating "arrogance". One who does not value others' time will be slowly and gradually socially boycotted. We all love to imitate the West and have picked so many cultural habits from them (wrong and right) but failed to pick up the good ones of being punctual, keeping schedules and respecting others' time. As a practice, I have reached venues/places on time without getting irritated, and people respect me for that alone.

We may at times feel "Why I should be on time when others are cominglate?" But believe me sooner or later others will start emulating us. Whenever I am invited toa function, the organisers know that when Suresh is invited, he will be on time and surely others follow and find that this habit actually gives all of us so much quality time to spend together. When I am invited as a Chief Guest for a function, the organisers start the programme on time which is appreciated by many.

Yet I am certain that there are a few people who are habitual late comers since either they like to make people wait or *like to be noticed when they walk in late.* Such people take pride in themselves but the others are generally irritated. Think of a person in our friend circle who ALWAYS reaches late. What do we think of such a person? Personally, I think it's an exhibition of arrogance. I would rather keep away from such persons and definitely, they would not be a part of my inner circle.

If we want to make things happen we need to be disciplined, proactive and self-starters. Then we shall be accountable, responsible, and trustworthy and respect others' time by being punctual.Isn't this professionalism at its best?

6

Acceptable and Approachable

Sixth Attribute to make Things Happen

Creating a nonthreatening environment

These two words are interrelated. Acceptability is when people like to speak to us, be with us and seek our company. And that is possible when we are approachable. These are qualities that can be seen in a few individuals. Their body language demonstrates that they are people-centred, acceptable and approachable. Especially,their facial expressions and modulation of voice.

Acceptability and Approachability are reflected when we have the ability to create a nonthreatening environment. In any role that we play—be it a father, mother, relative, sibling, son, daughter, grandparent, student, boss, peer or subordinate—it is possible to maintain a distance yet be acceptable and approachable. Yes, I understand that sometimes in a position of authority and as a leadership strategy one has to draw a limit and redefine the word "Approachable". But that is only situational.

I am tempted to refer to my father's example once again. He was a good man and provided everything for the family but all five brothers were afraid to speak to him, leave alone sit and discuss issues concerning our goals, our future etc. As a result, we brothers never had open discussions nor did our friends visit our house when my father was around. Probably, it was an Indian mindset in those times that 'Dads have to be like that'. Not anymore. Though there are a few dads like that even today, fortunately, their numbers are declining year after year, generation after generation.

I would probably equate people who are not approachable and hence not acceptable with 'arrogance'. One label I would never allow to be put on me. One bad episode or behaviour or body language and we are at the risk of being labelled as arrogant but once labelled it's very difficult to remove the same. People may respect us out of fear but an arrogant person's acceptability is very poor.

It is very unfortunate to sometimes see that as people grow in hierarchy or position or status they are more susceptible to acquiringthis label. During my 44 years in a medical school as a teacher, researcher, educationist, mentor and administrator, I have seen many people demonstrating arrogance with the increasing proportion as their hierarchical position in the organisation went on rising. It is not only common with position but also related to the job profile, department or field they are in. It somehow reflects in our body language and could be detrimental toour acceptability as a person or as a human being. So, a word of caution! Never allow the label of 'arrogance' to be tagged on us even when we are growing in position at the workplace, home or society.

How so ever great one becomes one has to be acceptable and approachable. The great statesman Late Prime Minister Atal Bihar Vajpayee was very deft in this virtue. He was acceptable to even the vehement opposition leaders. This virtue makes our lives easier.

We all have preferences of whom we are free with, Mom or Dad; there is nothing wrong with that. If someone had asked us this question when we were children, our instant answer would have been, "Of course, Mom!"Today, if someone asks a child, "Who are you more comfortable with? Dad or Mom?" The child takes a while to answer and the answer now is not a quick "Mom" because the child is no longer afraid of Dad. It's very heartening to see a child being equally comfortable with both parents and that's the right direction India is moving. But unfortunately, hierarchical arrogance still exists in workplaces. We will break this jinx. We shall be called acceptable and approachable.

One way of getting rid of this label and shedding our egos is by joining social organisations where we are practically taught to work without arrogance. It's here, we meet people belonging to various professions and hierarchies. If we have to survive in a social organization we have to learn very quickly to work with people of different statuses, strata and hierarchical positions with proper body language. That's how we learn to minimise our arrogance of position, colour or creed. Hence, I strongly recommend getting ourselves associated with any social organisation, not just as a status symbol member but as an active project manager. Life lessons are learnt when we work with different kinds of people. Man is a social animal, and if we are not social we remain animals!

If we want to make things happen then we need to be acceptable and approachable.

7

Apart: Being Creative and Innovative

Seventh Attribute to make Things Happen

Being Creative or Thinking out of the Box or doing Things Differently

Be different
make the difference

If we need to carve a niche for ourselves, we have to be very creative and innovative. We can apply the famous Kaizen technique to all facets of life and not alone to businesses. Steve Jobs was the best proponent of this virtue. This is a very useful weapon in our armoury.

There are two petrol pumps. At the first, the petrol pump attendant fills only petrol. At the other one, he fills petrol plus another attendant jumps forward to clean our windscreen without charging us extra. Which petrol pump would you like to go to?

There are two ice cream parlours. At one we get the regular ice cream cone. The other one gives us the cone with that very little extra scoop with a smile and offers tissues without our asking. Which ice cream parlour would we like to go to?

There are two vegetable vendors. One gives us correctly measured vegetables using a hand scale. Other weighs them using an electronic weighing machine and drops few coriander leaves in our basket without our asking. Which vendor would we prefer to go to?

There are two *pani puri* stalls (an Indian snack). The first one gives us eight *pani puris* as per his choice of flavour. The second one gives us eight, asking us after each *puri* if the sourness, sweetness and spice are good enough for our palate and gives that extra dry *puri* after the eighth *puri* on his own. Which stall would we visit the next time?

Creativity is doing the same thing differently. When I take out my wrist watch and hold it high in my hand and ask the participants in my programmes, "Apart from seeing time what are the different ways we can use this watch?"A few responses that I get are "Sir, for status, as an ornament, can sell and use the money, as a paper weight, to scratch, to play by throwing at each other, etc." We have never thought or trained our minds to think of the use of a wrist watch apart from showing time so it's initially difficult. But when few start thinking 'creatively and differently', others join in. Looking at the same object differently is creativity. Doing things differently is creativity.

All of us have this ability; it's only that we have never trained our minds to think differently, to think out of the box. We are so busy with mundane things in a typically routine way that our thinking is restricted to only 'that' way. People who apply this already existing ability outshine others, especially in competitive events or situations. I have heard of so many 'Out of the box' answers during various corporate interviews which show the quick presence of mind of the candidates, that one is inclined to select such candidates over others.

Recently I read this interview story which required a very different and rapid answer. The interviewer asked, "You are driving your car on a stormy day. You pass by a bus stop and see three people waiting there. The first is the perfect woman of your dreams. The second is an old friend who once saved your life and the third is an old lady who looks really sick. If you had only one seat in your car, whom would you offer a ride to?" This is a moral and ethical dilemma actually used as part of a job application. Do we pick the old woman because she is in critical condition and you should save her first? Do we take the old friend who once saved your life and this would be a perfect opportunity for you to pay him back? However, both choices leave you missing out on the woman of your dreams.

The candidate hired (out of 200 applicants) however, had no trouble answering. He simply said. "I would give the car keys to my old friend, let him drive the old lady to the hospital and I would stay behind to wait for the bus with the woman of my dreams." This answer completely changes our outlook and reminds us to always 'think out of the box'.

Everyone is born with capabilities and an instinct to be successful, but only the ones who think differently and out of the box succeed. Remember, big ideas come from forward-thinking people who challenge the norm, think outside the box, and invent the world they see inside rather than submit to the limitations of current dilemmas. As Arthur C Clarke said, "The limits of the possible can only be defined by going beyond them into the impossible". You will find many such creative answers in our Google search given in top interviews like in IAS or IIMs. They all stand apart and hence were selected.

If we want to make things happen then we need to demonstrate presence of mind or creativity, and out-of-the-box actions in day-to-day activities. We have to be *apart*.

8

Ambivert

Eighth Attribute to make Things Happen

To Understand this Ability of being an Ambivert: The Ability to Choose between Extrovert and Introvert Behaviour

Ability to choose between extrovert and introvert behavior

Extrovert and Introvert are two behaviours that we must have encountered around us at the workplace, at home or in social associations.

Before we start to analyse the two behaviours let me be clear that I am of the opinion that no behaviour is bad or good. And both exist in every person. I will explain this as we move forward. First, let us look at how these two behaviours are generally envisaged by people.

Extrovert	Introvert
Loves being with people	Likes to be alone and quiet
Ready to answer even before a question is complete	Answers only when asked
Huge social network	Prefers solitude
Enjoys being the centreof attention	Avoids being the centreof attention
Tends to think out loudly	Thinks before speaking
Loves being in a large group	Values close 1:1 relationship
Gains energy from being around with people	Prefers working in a quiet, independent environment
Outgoing, enthusiastic	Can be seen as reserved, shy

During my training sessions I ask participants individually what they think of their own behaviour.Are you an extrovert or an introvert? Some of them who are enthusiastic, bold, like to express and talk and want to be visible, label themselves as extroverts and some who are quiet and think that they are shy, call themselves introverts. But there are a few who cannot make up their mind and either say "I don't know,sir" or just keep quiet and smile without an answer. Then when I ask them which is a better behaviour there are very quick reactions that extroverts are better because they are more popular. It is interesting when I drag the discussion further and ask them what do they think of a 24 X 7 extrovert.I have generally found that the so-called introverts love to answer this question. They say, "Sir, such people who are 24 x 7 extroverts are sometimes irritating, talk too much, do not allow others (us) to talk, can hurt people and will never realise that they have done so. They are also dominating and overpowering". And what about 24 x 7 introverts? The answer is, "Sir, people do not like them much or want to be associated with such loners, shy people who do not want to be a part of anything. They are such a bore, sir."

But there is a choice. I can choose to be an extrovert or an introvert depending on the situation. That's what professionalism is. Think and tell me whom do we call an immature person? I think a person whose behaviour does not match the situation can be called immature. During a serious discussion if a person is behaving like a monkey, then surely there is a mismatch in behaviour and we call such a person immature. On the contrary, if the situation demands us to be a part of social interaction like dance or game and we do not take part in such activities just because we have labelledourselves as "introverts", we will be regarded as bore and will be socially boycotted.

If extrovert and introvert are two behaviours then ambivert is an ability. It's an ability to shift our behaviour from an extrovert to an introvert and vice versa depending on the situation without compromising on our core values. A person who has this ability is more acceptable and hence I regard this as an important attribute to make things happen.

Let me give an example. I used to be uncomfortable when invited to the dance floor during a party organised by my young students. As soon as I enter the party hall, an enthusiastic extrovert student comes running to me and invites me straight to the dance floor where the youngsters are dancing and enjoying. "Sir, please come and join us for a dance, we will love that". Though I am uncomfortable doing that because I feel I am not good at dancing, I still move out of my comfort zone and go to the dance floor for a few minutes and shake my legs a bit. I feel that if this action of mine can make so many people around me happy, then what is the problem? To switch for a few minutes from an introvert to an extrovert in this area of dancing that makes people happy is an ability. An ability to be flexible and switch from an introverted behaviour to an extrovert behaviour or vice versa and is called AMBIVERT.

Moreover, merely dancing for a few minutes is not going to infringe on my value system. They are not asking me to smoke, drink alcohol or do something that is coming between my core values. A few dance steps, that's all! I would happily do it for the sake of my participants if it does not come between me and my core values.

It is important to identify the situation and choose the behaviour. This is flexibility in behaviour.Ambiverts are more socially acceptable and also others are more comfortable working with such people. They are better team players and when required can emerge as better leaders. Hence, as I had mentioned earlier that both extroverts and introverts exist in a person. It's up to us to use the appropriate behaviour depending on the situation.

If we want to make things happen then we need to understand that there is nothing good or bad about being an extrovert or an introvert as long as it matches the situation.

9

Active Speaker

The Ninth Attribute can we "Express to Impress"?

Express to Impress

"World can only know how much you know when you present effectively"

This expectation of people from us is debatable. But during all my group discussions and interview skills workshops with engineering and MBA students, I noticed that students who have theability to express themselves or are capable to make powerful presentations have a definite edge over others. Of course, content is the most important. But what good is the sea of contents when we cannot present our thoughts in a manner to impress others, especially in a group discussion or interview?Knowledge unless expressed effectively is of no use. One of the basic necessities to excel is to develop one`s presentation skills. And hence I am tempted to elaborate on this attribute.

"The human mind is a wonderful thing. It operates from the moment you are born until the time you get up to make a presentation."

I remember a certain surgery postgraduate student Dr Sagar, who had secured a great rank in his PG entrance exam. In his first year of Residency, he showed excellent surgical skills and was brilliant in his academics. He was excited when he was involved in a classical clinical case. Then came the trauma, when he was asked to present this case in the clinical meeting of the institute. His guide, Dr Sudhir came to me and said, "Suresh,sir, I am worried about this PG student of mine who no doubt, is a brilliant student but of late very nervous since he has been asked to make a presentation," He continued, "His PPT`s are good but when I heard him yesterday, he was visibly shaking and was fumbling with words. You are involved with speaking skills regularly, please do something."

I smiled and said, "Sudhir, these are very common symptoms and such butterflies are experienced by everyone, only the size and the quantum differ from people to people, don't you worry, presentation is a skill and if it is a skill it can be learnt. Sachin Tendulkar, the great cricket legend was not born with a bat in his hand. He learnt this skill the hard way. Give me a week with this PG student of yours, send him to our Communication Skill Lab and let's see what can be done. Sure enough, when the day came Sagar did a fairly good job and this is what he had to say, "Sir, thanks for your guidance and support, if not anything else, my confidence was good. Next time it will be better."

Presentation is a Skill and it can be Learnt

To have knowledge is one thing and to have the skill to deliver that knowledge in front of colleagues and experts either at home or in a conference (public) is another. But as I have said earlier, if it's a skill it can be learnt and mastered slowly. The art of making a powerful presentation is coachable and every time we get up to make a presentation we can see success when we look at the eyes of our audience. We enjoy doing this again and again and it just grows on us. And then it becomes a habit and people just love to listen to us.

In the following pages, I am sharing my experience of the several public speaking and presentation skills workshops that I have conducted for youth and adults. These are just tips to make our presentation powerful. However, it is how we practice them and add our own creativity that will make themall the more powerful. But the principles remain the same whether you are a CEO or a student or a faculty making a presentation ata conference or a public function.

1. Butterflies in the Stomach

All of us have felt them the first time we went on the platform for a presentation. During a survey conducted on the **ten worst human fears in the USA, the** following was the result:

10. Dogs

09. Loneliness

08. Flying

07. Death

06. Sickness

05. Deep Waters

04. Financial Problems

03. Insects & Bugs

02. Heights

01. Speaking before an audience

Dogs were feared the least and the worst fear was facing an audience. This just goes to say that stage fright is natural and everyone experiences it at one time or the other.

Have We Experienced these Symptoms of STAGE-FRIGHT?

Rapid heartbeat, trembling knees, quivering voice, stomach fluttering, blurring of eyes, sweating on hands, dryness in the mouth, faster breathing, mind going blank-thought block, voice cracking, flop sweat (one small drop of sweat that drains down your vertebral column), which leads to embarrassment-panic-shame humiliation-fear.

If we have experienced any of the above, don't worry. These are natural common symptoms and we are not alone.

12 Most Common Reasons for a such Fright are Fear of

1. Failure: what if I fail, if the electricity goes off, slides stop working

2. Ridicule/humiliation: what if someone laughs?

3. Presence of some persons like a boss, peer, known or unknown

4. Criticism or critical evaluation

5. Incompetence of language

6. Exposure of thoughts, emotions

7. Loss of relationships

8. Concern of consequence

9. Own voice

10. Crowd-people

11. Competition

12. Lack of knowledge

STEPS TO CONTROL STAGEFEAR:

1. Choose a subject that we strongly wish to discuss with our audience

2. Prepare and practice thoroughly

3. Recognise that we are not alone in suffering from stagefear

4. Realise that we appear more confident than we feel

5. Understand that with the experience our stage fear will be reduced

6. Know that the audience wants us to perform well

7. Remember there will always be a next time

Now let's go through these four important steps while making a presentation,

1. **Audience analysis**

2. **Designing and organising the contents**

3. **Adding style to the presentation**

4. **Evaluating or looking for feedback**

1. Audience Analysis

The **most important step** for a powerful presentation is an analysis of the audience. Before we sit and assemble our contents we should be able to get an answer to the five Ws that will decide the final H (How).

1. WHO are these people? What is their level? Their gender and age? Which language do most of them understand? How many are they (number), and what is their attitude towards us and the subject we wish to speak about?

2. WHAT kind of presentation or speech is that? Entertaining, Informative, Motivational, Introduction, Welcome, Farewell, Thanksgiving, Winners or Losers Speech, Conveying good or bad news, etc.

3. WHEN: what time of the day is our presentation? Is it before breakfast, pre-lunch, post-lunch, in the evening just before the cocktails and dinner or during the dinner? Also, the duration of our speech, how much time have we been given by the organisers?

4. WHERE: Location and ambience/surroundings, closed auditorium with or without air-conditioner, open area, lawn or garden with a lot of distractions or is it in a state-of-the-art conference hall with excellent acoustics.

5. Finally, WHY? Why have we been chosen to speak? Is it because we are an expert or is it a competition of sorts and why now, is there a special occasion?

Once we seek answers for these five Ws then we can sit back and decide HOW, the H.

Your designing of the presentation largely depends on your audience analysis. We must have realised that if 'WHO' changes, 'HOW' will also change. Our content and skill will differ depending on whether we are speaking in front of peers or seniors or mixed groups or nonprofessionals or people more knowledgeable than us about the subject or less knowledgeable or college students or school children or slum dwellers or competent professionals. If the presentation fails, it's almost always because the speaker didn't frame it correctly in accordance with the need of the audience or just misjudged the audience's level of interest or knowledge.

Hence personally, I give a lot of importance and time to analyse myaudience before I design my presentation.

2. Designing and Organising the Contents

There's no way we can present a good talk unless we have something worth talking about. Conceptualising and framing what we want to say is the most vital part of preparation.

While designing the HOW, we should divide the presentation into three parts

The opening (15%)

The body (75%) and

The closing (10%)

All that takes the audience through a journey.

A. The Opening

The beginning of our presentation is crucial. We need to grab our audience's attention and hold it!

A good opening is key before we launch ourselves into the main content area. These initial moments set the momentum and connect us with the audience. How much time we spend on the opening is decided by the total time allotted to us but not more than 12-15%.

I have personally realised that many times it is important to sit through the presentation of the previous speakers and pick up from where they have left in the opening lines of our presentation. Exciting openings are recommended in post-lunch sessions or if we feel the audience has slept through the previous session even in an academic presentation.

In any case, a solid start is a launch pad for our subsequent minutes of delivery of the presentation. If we start by using jargon or get too technical, we will lose them. Once we lose our audience it is very difficult to bring them back. The most powerful presenters do a superb job of introducing the topic in an effective manner, explaining why they care so deeply about it and convincing the audience that they should be doing the same.

An opening should announce that you have arrived!

- They are also called icebreakers or de-freezers.

- They are attention-getters and should arouse interest.

- They could be illustrations, couplets, questions, exhibits, shocking facts, storiesor just a smile.

- They may start with Salutations (addressing the people on the dais and off the dais)

B. The Body

Making the purpose of the speech explicit and clear is the basic task of the body of the presentation. No hard and fast rules may be given for the arrangement of the ideas and the construction of the speech body since each speech presents its own problems. For an effective presentation, simple and logical development of the speech is a must.

- Arrange the main points logically with data support

- Think-Observe-Read-Converse-Interview

- Meant to clarifythe purpose of the presentation

- Use concrete examples, facts and figures

- Simple logical development to be completed within time.

- Use creative appropriate humour. Use cue cards

- Avoid abstract and generalised statements with too many technical words

If we want to make our presentation stand out from the rest, we have to focus on creating a well-designed, visually pleasing presentation filled with convincing data and a narrative structure that resonates.

Think about how we are going to share facts and figures. If we are showing a trend or comparison, then a well-constructed line graph or bar chart may be all that's required to make our point. Be cautious while using pie charts though. It's not easy to make sense of abstract angles and it gets worse if there are lots of segments.

Consider our use of text carefully. I recently saw a presentation bya faculty with 278 words on a single slide. Yes, I counted. And no, I'm still not sure what their message was. Maybe because I was busy counting! Use text sparingly and use a large, clear font. It can be useful for quotes or to emphasise a point that we have just made. Just remember that our audience can't read and listen to us at the same time, so always pause after revealing something on the screen.

Use animation with caution in a PowerPoint presentation. Academic presentations should not have cartoon characters dropping in and out of the slide every time we change the slide. Avoid showing all the text at the same time because when we speak about the first point, the audience is reading our last line. So, the best thing is to use custom animation to reveal one line at a time.In any case, **keep it simple**.

C. The closing

The closing should be gradual, not abrupt. We should avoid saying, "I have nothing else to say, so I think I will stop now". It should be as logical as the body that should gradually merge with building a climax with time in mind.

Purpose of a good closing:

- Summarising and restating-outlining main points covered in the speech

- Making a memorable statement that should be remembered for a long time

- Appealing for action

- Paying a sincere compliment to the audience

3. Adding Style to the Presentation

Nonverbal cues can either make or break a good presentation. Remember, the audience is not only reading with us and listening to what we are saying but isalso actively involved in looking at us. **Anything that distracts the audience can be dangerous** since the audience spends most of its time focusing on these distractions rather than our presentation.

In fact, we are judged even before we begin to speak. No sooner our name is announced all eyes are on us, so take special care. Walk gracefully since we are under scrutiny.

Elements like dress sense (what we wear), posture (how we stand and move), gesture (movements of hands), facial expression, eye contact, language, listening cues and modulation of voice could be support systems that could make our presentation exemplary or could be distracters taking the focus of the audience away from our presentation.

Dress sense: Dress to the occasion. Both we and the audience should feel comfortable with what we wear. There is nothing wrong withlooking good and it is important, but avoid excess makeup and flashy dress for an academic or professional presentation. It is safe to wear formal clothes. A dress that does not match the occasion may distract the audience. Smart attire radiates confidence.

Posture: It's important how we stand and move. If it is a podium presentation our movements may be restricted, but when there is the freedom to move, then remember to make small but not brisk or fast movements. While standing, it's best to keep our feet several inches apart, our body well balanced, and non-rocking with a natural lean. As a speaker, do not sway and this can be avoided if we make a conscious effort to stand with our body weight equally divided on both of our feet.

Gesture: Parking of the hand is always a problem. Some presenters have this habit of moving their hands in a peculiar manner or keeping their hands in their pockets or playing with the keys in their hands or pocket or using a particular word repeatedly. I have seen the audience busy counting the number of times the word was repeated or action was repeated. The focus shifts from the presentation to the presenter.

Subtle movements of the hand while making a point, and making the right gesture to emphasise the word add power to the presentation. Gestures should be natural, easy and spontaneous and match the thinking and the words that are spoken. Avoid too many, too large, too frequent and busy movements of the hands so that it does not appear too dramatic. In short, avoid distracting mannerisms.

Facial Expression: This should be congruent with the spoken words. Smile when there is a touch of humour to be added. Keep your expressions firm when there is a serious matter to be placed. Even while thanking people, the face should reflect 'Thank you'. Face should be animated, alert, intelligent, pleasing, enthusiastic, smiling and relaxed. One thing which should be very clearly seen on the speaker's face is the enthusiasm for the job he is doing as it will be passed on to the audience.

Eye Contact: Good eye contact makes every individual feel as if we are addressing him/her. Eye contact makes the person feel more important. A strong bond is established between the audience and the speaker by maintaining good eye contact. The advantage of good eye contact is that it reflects the confidence of the speaker. Eye contact if properly used helps the speaker to gauge the acceptance of his idea as the first reaction shown by the audience is through his/her eye. So, if proper eye contact is there, the presenter can change, modify, correct or alter his style and idea to convince the audience.

In fact, a smart presenter uses eye contact for multiple purposes like feedback, gaining attention, increasingacceptance, bringing back the non-attentive, etc. In any case, I strongly recommend we avoid a fixed gaze and while addressing a large gathering we should not follow a pattern but the eye movements should be random and sweeping.

Language: Although it is recommended to use a single language, my personal experience encourages the use of English, Hindi and regional language in bits and pieces. Simple language without jargon is largely accepted by the audience. Care should be taken to spell-check all slides in our presentation and look for any grammatical mistakes.

Listening Cues: When a question is asked or someone is answering in the audience, take time and demonstrate good listening skills. This will encourage the audience to connect with us and respond better.

Modulation of voice: All the above style skills are of no use without proper modulation of voice. Modulation includes voice pitch, pace, pause and emphasis. I remember my school English teacher givingme paragraphs from speeches of eminent scholars and leaders and askingme to read them several times with a challenge that each time the modulation should be different.

The power of a powerful presentation strongly circles around how good is our modulation. When to raise our voice, which word to emphasise, and letting our voice rise and fall at the appropriate moment. Speed, not too fast or too slow, givesintervals between words, ideas, and sentences to enable the listener to absorb, register, and assimilate and also enables us to breathe. Modulation makes our voice appealing to the listeners and offers emotions in different shades to your presentation.

"They may forget what you said, but they will never forget how you made them feel". Carl W Buechner

4. Evaluating or Looking for Feedback

A careful look at the audience will no doubt informally tell us if our presentation has been successful, but we need to have formal feedback channels to evaluate our performance. After our presentation, there will be several known and unknown persons who will come to us and say "Sir, your presentation today was too good, excellent, never heard before, etc., etc." But I would think twice before believing them all. Some may be genuine, which we will be able to recognise only with experience. I strongly recommend cultivating or nurturing a feedback partner, someone who will give honest critical criticism about content and style. I know this is easier said than done. But surely this helps us in our next presentation.

"I am the most spontaneous speaker in the world because every word, every gesture, and every retort has been carefully rehearsed". George Bernard Shaw

MIKE: Devil or friend?

1. Imagine a speech without a mike. It helps us throw our voices. So always use a mike.

2. I would recommend a collar mike since it leaves our hands free for gestures.

3. Take time to adjust the mike. Keep the mike at a level below our lips and its midpoint in level with the chin. Check that the mike does not cover our faces. Adjust ourselves to the mike.

4. Distance approximately one fist full (depending on the quality of the mike)

5. Do not start till we are sure the mike system works well.

6. Do not shout but speak naturally in the mike.

7. Don't worry if our own voice sounds queer or changed.

TIPS FOR A POWERFUL PRESENTATION

1. Thoroughly analyse our audience

2. Simple language, unadulterated

3. Avoid too much history and statistics

4. Clarity of thoughts before the presentation

5. Use cue cards. Avoid memorizing, and reading

6. Don't be sarcastic, sentimental, or exaggerated

7. Eat sparingly before a speech

8. Develop reading and habit of discussions on issues

9. Be on time

10. Do not start with an apology

11. Do not conclude abruptly

12. **Practice, practice and practice with our feedback partner.**

"There are always three speeches for each one that you actually gave

- *The one we practised*

- *The one we gave*

- *The one we wish we gave"*

– Dale Carnegie

If we want to make things happen then we need to master this very important skill of presenting our thoughts, ideas and opinions in front of people.

10

Assertive Communication

The Tenth Attribute to make Things Happen:

Assertive Communication

with Rationality and Empathy

Being firm yet polite.
Telling what is in your mind
without hurting

The growth and development of mankind havebeen possible mainly due to communication between human beings. Try as we may, it is not possible to stop communication between people because it is essential to life. Communication is basically a human dialogue. It is a social skill. Without it, mankind has no chance for progress. In spite of technological advancements in communication, there is still a communication gap, a breakdown between people and units of people. This breakdown is a sharp reminder that communication is a human skill and not a technical skill. Hence, the need for every human being to know and practice it to make it all the better for you to interact with people infamily, workplace, and society.

Assertive Communication

The most effective method to use while trying to accomplish our communication goal is the assertive approach.There are several situations in life when we have to be assertive. That is, being firm yet polite. Especially in difficult situations with difficult people. Even in several common situations at home, workplace or in society we need to say 'NO' or 'Refuse' certain demands of people or 'make a point' with people. This is where Assertive Communication helps. Expressing what we want to say 'Without hurting people'. It also means letting people know what our priorities, preferences, wants, and needs are in a special situation while allowing them to state theirs and taking them into account.

Characteristics of Assertive Communication is a five-step approach

1. An appropriate opening in a **non-threatening environment**

2. Using receiver-friendly simple language with **rationality**

3. Understanding emotions (**empathy**)

4. **Assertive communication skills** with proper body language

5. Active **listening skills**

Use each of these, every time you encounter a person. 'Every time' may sound difficult since there are some difficult persons in certain difficult situations. But with practice and repeated behaviour the same becomes a habit and we start subconsciously using these five steps.

The way we start a conversation depends on many factors. Who is the person? What am I going to speak? Is it the appropriate time and place? In any case, the opening is crucial and will be a platform to create a **non-threatening environment**. Communication and reaching out to people are easier when the atmosphere is calm, easy and normal.

It also helps a great deal when there is logic or reasoning in what we are saying. I mean there is **rationality**. Few words or sentences explaining why and what of the matter increases the chances of making the receiver listen to us more intently and reasonably.

The next step that may seem difficult during communication is understanding the emotions of others i.e.,**empathy**. Let me make it simple. Empathy is the skill of knowing what the other person feels without that person actually telling you! Empathy is 'feeling with' the person while sympathy is 'feeling for' the person. Empathy is a cerebral response while sympathy is a visceral response. Empathy is having and demonstrating concern for others. Empathy involves action.

For example, if we have had a cut on our hand which is bleeding profusely, so much so that we cannot talk and if a person who meets us says, "Oh my God,sir! Look how much you are bleeding. Must be painful,sir? And,sir, it's your right hand! Surely that's bad!" This is sympathy when this person is only attaching tothe situation. However, if a person runs and brings a bandage and gives us first aid on his or her own or rushes us to the casualty of a hospital without our asking, that's empathy, which involves attaching tothe situation and ACTION. Feeling concerned for others and doing exactly what the other person wants us to do without being asked is the highest order of emotional intelligence called empathy. Concern for others is the first step that leads to understanding the feelings of others and then acting in accordance.

Here is a 15 points inventory of acts. If we are saying YES for any of them, then we are NOT having concern for others or are LOW on empathy

DO WE

1. Throw garbage at will from our balcony/moving car

2. Spit as if the country is a spittoon

3. Write our name on monuments' walls/train toilets with a heart sign

4. Leave the tap open while brushing/shaving

5. Park our car in front of a store to enable our wife/mother/sister to shop and in the process block the road

6. Eve tease/comment/look down upon women

7. Do not take care of old people at home

8. Break traffic rules: lights, overtaking

9. Feel that some jobs are for women: Cleaning/ dishes / clothes, etc.

10. Use mobile phone at petrol pump/hospital

11. Block the main road while dancing in the marriage procession of our friend/relative

12. In the name of enjoyment talk loudly/sing till late at night along with our friends while travelling on a train

13. Shout and make life miserable in a hotel corridor where we have maximum rooms booked without caring for a few other occupants staying in rooms that have not been allotted to us

14. Blow the horn when not required

15. Take our dog for poop at the neighbour's gate

All of them are simple acts in our daily life that tell us if we are concerned about others. Are we emphatic towards others?

Empathy is a magic word and we must train our minds to consciously master this skill. Once we master this skill, we will start communicating with ease because we know exactly how the other person would feel when we speak or when we don't speak. We will know which language to speak and our communication will be both sensitive and sensible. We will also be calmer and have less stress. Put yourself in the receiver`s shoes for a better understanding of Empathy.

The most important step that has to be used more carefully in any communication encounter is **being assertive** which means being FIRM yet POLITE.

Let us understand these two wonderful words "Being Assertive"

Each one of us has assertive rights.

Right to

- Express our behaviour, thoughts, values and emotions

- Offer no reason for our behaviour

- Judge the extent to which we are responsible to others

- Change our minds andmake mistakes

- Say, "I don't know". Say, "No". Say, "I don't understand".

- Be treated with respect. Tell what we expect

- Get angry

- Ask for emotional support

- Protest unfair treatment. Ask for information

- Protest unfair criticism. And to criticise.

- To have an opinion

- To be listened to and taken seriously

- Say, "I love you/I hate you"

This is our personal bill of assertive rights. How we use these rights is assertiveness.

To exert our rights, inany given situation, we have a choice to react in three different ways. Either we can be aggressive or passive or simply assertive.

Let me give you a few examples.

We go to a restaurant and order Paneer Butter Masala (a very common Indian vegetarian dish). When the waiter brings this dish, we find that there is no paneer. What is our assertive right? We have the right to call the waiter and question him. We have the right to return the dish. We also have the right to ask for a refund.

How will an aggressive person react? This person will throw a lot of tantrums, shout at the waiter, throw abuses, demand that the waiter should call the manager, make a lot of noise, and create a scene till his rights are fulfilled.

How will a passive person react? This person may try to call the waiter and ask about the missing paneer very timidly but when the waiter starts manipulating with explanations this person will look down and start eating the dish ignoring his right, lest a scene is created. He will, in fact, ask the aggressive to keep quiet and eat whatever is available. They will feel sorry for themselvesthat such events always happen to them, get hurt and sulk.

How will an assertive person react? This person will call the waiter and politely yet firmly ask for an immediate replacement. Will not get manipulated by the explanations of the waiter and keeping his smile intact will demand a quick replacement of the dish.

Outcomes of these Three Behaviours

AGGRESSIVENESS results in temporary Success. Is expressed with anger and such a person is regarded as arrogant. People start maintaining social distance. Your rights are fulfilled BUT there is definitely a loss of relationships.

Aggression involves:

- Expression of emotions, but inappropriately and in violation of the rights of others.

- There is NO EMPATHY and there is an attempt to put other people down. Dominate others.

- Being a winner always while other people lose

- There is no rationality,no explanations

- Ignoring the wishes of others

- Getting annoyed and losing my temper

- Work is done but with a loss of relationships

- 'I win you lose' is the philosophy with which this reaction is associated

The option of becoming aggressive is tempting as it gives quick results but I would never recommend that style. We may get fast results by being aggressive but we will definitely compromise on relationships.

PASSIVE behaviour leaves us with a feeling of being lousy, guilty, 'I wish I had' and 'Why is God so unfair and unkind to me only' sort of thoughts. Such a person eventually gets a feeling of being used as a doormat. Rights are not fulfilled and the person will lose their relationship with self, which results in feeling overworked, stressed, angry and frustrated.

Passivity involves

- Being eager to please others all the time

- Always feeling that we may hurt people. "What will THEY think?" is uppermost in their minds.

- Being unwilling to say NO. Always apologising for own actions

- Always avoiding conflicts

- Always thinking that other people are right, and they are wrong

- They usually hide their feelings and are not able to address or use their rights

- There is a fear to perform anything with fear of failure, ridicule, humiliation, consequences, losing relationships, criticism and the presence of some people.

- Easily influenced by others

- Effects: Sulk later/after the episode. Doormat feeling. Being used.

- Self-pity leadsto frustration and anger (kept inside)

- Work not done with Loss of relationships and let down feeling of self

- 'I lose you win' is the philosophy with which this reaction is associated.

ASSERTIVENESS is an honest, polite, firm, confident and relaxed way of communication, where our rights are fulfilled keeping our relationship with people still healthy.

Assertiveness involves

- Self-worth. (I have the right!)

- Making our views clear and our voice heard

- Making our point. Tell what is in our mind

- Standing up for ourselves without losing our temper

- Negotiating terms that both find acceptable

- Without putting another person down

- Without making other people feel that they have lost

- FIRM YET POLITE. Using appropriate body language, gestures, facial expression, eye contact, language, and modulation of the voice in accordance with the situation and the person.

- 'I win; you also win' is the philosophy with which this reaction is associated.

Let us REACT!! Which is the best or worst?

Aggressive: work done but a loss of a relationship

Passive: work not done and loss of self-worth

Assertive: work done and relationships intact

Yes, the best is being assertive. But rightly, it's not being aggressive but being passive, which is the worst. Because when we are aggressive, at least we are fighting for our rights. A passive person is not only ignoring his/her right but in the process is constantly hurting oneself.

Depending on the situation and people, have we not expressed one or the other kind of behaviour?

The Key: we may use any reaction but the question is without getting hooked to passivity and aggressiveness, how quickly we get back to assertion? There may have been a situation where we may have been aggressive for some unavoidable reasons. But emotionally intelligent people realise that they have reacted aggressively or passively and do not get hooked on to that particular behaviour and return to assertion quickly. However, it is not conducive toeffective communication when a person gets into the habit of being aggressive or passive in all situations and with all people.

Special Mention of a Very Familiar Passive Behaviour

Saying YES when you want to say NO!

NO in the mind but YES on the lips!!

One fine morning my best friend's wife came home and she seemed to be very disturbed. After a while, she could not control her emotions and broke down saying, "Your friend, my husband does not have time for me and our family. Anybody walks into our house and off he goes with them for their work which sometimes is very trifle and unimportant. He understands that their errands are not the top priority for him yet he refuses to say NO. The word NO does not seem to be in his dictionary".I tried to pacify her by giving her a glass of water but she continued speaking with intermittent sobs, "This has been happening with repeated frequency and is now affecting his health. His eating habits and timings have changed leading to acidity and he has of late become very irritable. I think people are using him and taking advantage ofhim as he cannot refuse anyone. Suresh, you are his good friend and counsellor. Please help before it's too late"

How many times have we thought of saying NO but end up saying YES?

NO means NO. But why is saying NO so difficult for some?

Here are some typical perceptions that people have when they are saying YES when actually they want to say NO:

Others will get annoyed with me.

People will feel bad or hurt.

They will feel I am letting them down, I am being rude or selfish.

I am known for saying Yes. So how can I say NO?

They will think I am arrogant.

They may think I am not friendly.

If it's the boss: I might lose the job, and lose his/her trust.

Can't say No since it's my job so I have to do it!

I may find it difficult to ask for favour from them in future.

I will become unpopular.

I am popular and liked because I never say NO.

I may lose a good relationship.

If these are happening, then STOP saying yes always.

Are you getting a reputation forbeing a 'doormat'?

Are you getting a feeling 'GOD, why only me'?

Are you becoming overworked or stressed?

Are you finding no time for your own work and family leading to frustration?

Do you have hidden resentments against people who keep asking you for unreasonable favours?

Are you losing your temper, at soft targets at home/workplace?

Are you becoming more aggressive?

If any of the above is happening toyou, then it's time to stop and think. At what cost am I getting drawn into this passive mode of saying YES when I should be saying NO that is adversely affecting my life and that of my near and dear ones?

Remember you have the right to say NO, but assertively

- An aggressive NO is an offensive No. It clearly communicates NO, however it also offends/hurts the other person and shows no concern for others.

- Passive NO. Weak No. Accompanied bylots of excuses andjustifications. The whole scene may turn too complicated. You do not want to displease. End up crying/feeling frustrated or low

- Assertive NO. Saying NO without hurting. Needs courage of conviction and & skills

The use of "I" statements while dealing with parents, elders, seniors, and people in authority will make the communication more assertive and will make you at ease to say NO. Begin with

I feel,

I think,

I want you to…

I need,

I understand.…

I am Upset about…

I would prefer…

Listen, I said NO (in extreme situations)

Assertively saying "No" involves

Honesty, self-respect, good body language

You can also try any of these:

"I can do some of the work now, rest later" Is it ok?

"If you can help me with it, I will do it"

"If you do *this* for me, I will be glad to do *that*"

"I can`t do it, but let me find someone who can"

"I can`t help much, but let's work out together how the task can be done"

"Can I do it tomorrow?"

"I am really sorry, this time I can`t do it"

"We can do it together"

Active listening is keeping distractions to the minimum while listening. It also means paying attention even if we disagree and being nonjudgmental. Good listeners demonstrate that they are actively listening by giving nonverbal cues, which also tell the sender that the receiver is open to new thoughts and ideas. It is a good idea to give space and repeat (paraphrase) what the sender says while in conversation. I strongly recommend training ourselves to be good listeners since active listening is the strongest element to make our assertive communication effective. Think about this 'Only a good receiver can be a good sender'.

If we train ourselves to master active listening, we are actually good at empathy and hence in the natural course of time reject aggression and adapt to assertive communication. The result of all these is that we are able to create a **non-threatening environment** that is conducive toeffective communication.

In Short

The ability to influence and manage our own and others' emotions is essential in most aspects of human relations, in both social contacts and in more informal settings like home. Think for a moment about what kind of life it would be without these social skills and how serious the consequences would be.

If we lack assertive skills, including an inability to say NO, we may find ourselves taken advantage of and unable to defend ourselves. Passive people end up feeling that they arebeing taken advantage of. This produces timidity and social anxiety which leads us to avoid social situations. This in turn leads to poor self-esteem and feeling of being unwanted. Aggression on the other hand may give quick results (and hence tempting to use again and again) but is the main reason for spoilt relationships. Outright aggression may be useful in certain provocative situations but is never recommended. Hence being assertive commands respect and helps in managing good and healthy relationships with everyone around.

Being assertive does not mean getting our own way all the time or always listening to others or manipulating people; it is an alternate method of behaviour which leads to a win-win situation for both parties.

Worksheet 1

Can you handle these situations assertively?

Think what would be the result if the same situations were handled by you aggressively OR in a passive manner.

1. Saree salesman shows you many items but you do not like any! Yet, you buy something.

2. You are in a hurry to reach work/college when at the petrol pump you meet a friend/senior who says "*Aur suna yaar*" or says "Please join me for a cup of coffee".

3. Your friend's sister visits your house asking you to buy some expensive but good products (encyclopaedia, children's books, network products, etc.). You do not want to buy anything.

4. You are standing at a counter in a railway reservation queue. Suddenly a man jumps the queue.

5. Your parents are looking for a match for you. But you are already in a serious relationship with someone you dearly love.

6. You buy a dress. The washing instructions are followed. It still shrinks. You ask for your money back. The shopkeeper says this has never happened before and insists that you have washed wrongly.

7. Your friend has borrowed money/book/something precious from you many months earlier. You want it urgently now.

8. Your parents have retired from their work and are ageing. You have been offered by your company your dream position outside your city away from your parents. You are guilty of leaving them.

9. Your teacher unexpectedly asks you to stay back for a Project when you have other plans with your close friends.

10. Friends try to get you to have one drink/smoke/*hukka* even though you have refused them several times

11. School children ask for a donation for a social cause. You have contributed to the same earlier elsewhere.

12. You are in a washroom of an expensive restaurant. The attendant holds a towel and looks at you expectantly. You don't have to change for a tip.

13. You have just dined with your friends in a restaurant and you have not tipped or under-tipped the waiter. He runs after you to hand over your jacket which you have forgotten.

14. You have fixed an outing with your friend well in advance. Now your parents want you to attend a family reunion/marriage of your relative with them on the same day.

15. You are on a road trip with your friends and need to use the washroom. You stop at a petrol pump, but you do not need any petrol.

16. You and your friend (both females) are walking down a 'not so busy' street. Two street boys pass nasty comments.

17. A boy known to you from a good family approaches you and wants you to go out with him. You do not want to.

Bottom Line

- **How** we say is more important than **what** we want to say.

- We may go to aggression or passivity depending on the situation and people. But don't get hooked on to them andquickly come back to assertion.

- To be assertive we need to create a non-threatening environment using rationality, empathy andactive listening.

- Assertiveness is a skill and it can be learnt and mastered.

If we want to make things happen then we must include these three principles of human relations in all our conversations; rationality, empathy and assertiveness.

11

Appreciation

The Eleventh Attribute to make Things Happen

Appreciation or Recognition: The Fourth Basic Human Need

Appreciation
Genuine, Immediate and Timely

Yet another area where we need to work to demonstrate concern for others (empathy) is appreciation or recognition.

Since childhood, we have been hearing of three basic human needs food, clothing and shelter. I am tempted to add the fourth dimension 'recognition' or need to be appreciated.

Let me give a few examples,

1. Every morning, my 92-year-old mother walks very slowly 30 times up and down her 15 x 20 sq.ft. room using a walker. Today she did it 35 times and was excited about it and almost shouted from her room "Look Suresh, today I have done it 35 times". What is she expecting me to reply?

2. My one and half-year-old granddaughter werecrawling till yesterday. Today she gets up on her two legs and manages four steps before she falls but instead of crying, looks up in excitement. What is she expecting me to say?

3. My 35-year-old son drives home his new car and calls out aloud "Let's all go for a drive" What is he expecting me to say?

4. My 55 years old sister-in-law known for her expertise in trying new cuisines makes an exceptionally new special dish for dinner and serves us. She involuntarily waits for a few seconds near our table. What is she expecting me to say?

5. My junior colleague makes a very good presentation today about our department. After the presentation, he hurriedly comes near me and looks at me. What is he expecting me to say?

6. My boss announces an increment and some 'goodies' for all the employees for the upcoming festival and waits for a while before continuing his speech. What is he expecting us to say?

7. When the husband or wife takes all the time to wear a new dress and walks into the drawing room where we are waiting to go out for a party. What are they expecting us to say?

8. My neighbour's daughter is selected for the National Tennis team. This announcement was made just today morning. I happen to meet her outside across the road. What is she expecting me to say?

9. My housemaid does a good job using her indigenous powder to clean our house brass articles. She brings them all into the drawing hall and looks up with a smile. What is she expecting me to say?

10. When I stroll into our small personal garden the sincere old-time gardener is softly touching the plants and proudly looking at the flowers. What is he expecting me to say?

The answer toall the similar questions is 'appreciation'. The expression of appreciation can be different in different situations and for different people. In some examples, there is an expectation to at least lookup or give some silent cue that we like it. In some, there could be applause, or simply give a smile of approval.

All these expectations are natural and normal. All may not express or ask for appreciation in so many words but believe me we all like it when we are appreciated for the right thing at the right time and place. Hence I call it the 'fourth basic human need'.

Appreciating people for a job well done is a skill and an important attribute in personal growth and making people grow. It's a leadership skill to correctly assess which person or situation needs to be appreciated and more so 'how' to show appreciation. Organizational policies of appreciation in the form of rewards, recognitions and incentives go a long way in building trust and motivation amongst the employees. This act of appreciation is applicable to everyone, to all people in any hierarchal position.

This is true for all of us at the home, workplace and in society. We are all a part of this social system and must be sensitive about this need to be appreciated and hence we should generously express the same during our interaction with people. One of the important characteristics of a strong personality is the ability to understand this need of people and master the art of appreciation that has to be genuine, immediate and timely, to the right person at the right time and the right place.

If we want to make things happen then we need to master this skill of appreciating people; the right people at the right time and place. This skill can be mastered if we have concern for people and empathise with them.

FINALLY

12

Do we have a Feedback Partner?

Do you have a feedback partner?

I would finally like to end with this all-important question.

Do we have a feedback partner?

They are also called follow-up partners or fallback partners.

For all the twelve attributes to be a reality, we need someone to tell us that we are going in the right direction. I call them feedback partners. They are all around us but we miss out on them or fail to recognise their presence. They may be anyone; father, mother, brother, sister, uncle, aunt, friend, teacher, guide or mentor. There is no restriction of age, gender, community or creed to be a feedback partner. There is a mutual feeling of compassion towards each other. Generally, feedback partners are people belonging to our inner circle, whom we can fall back upon and who always wish for our welfare and want us to succeed.

These are people to whom we have given the authority to hold us by the collar and shake us when we are not doing the right thing or straying away from our goal, hurting people or simply not showing the right kind of behaviour for the given situation. They are also the same people who appreciate us when we do good, give approval for our stand when we demonstrate assertive behaviour and stand like a rock while we are pursuing our goals.

They are people who do not expect anything in return and have unconditional love towards us. They do not fear reprimanding or appreciating us and it is *expected* that we in return demonstrate the same. I fully understand that it may not always be possible to reciprocate, but there should remain a strong feeling of genuine caring for each other. It is a mutual unwritten agreement.

Once we identify the persons as our feedback partners, we should try to nourish this relationship and never lose them. They are valuable assets and have to be kept beside us all through our life. I have had participants who have said that they have multiple feedback partners for different areas of their life like workplace, family relationships and social encounters.

Giving and receiving feedback both are complex processes. Some people will find giving feedback difficult and most feel receiving as difficult. That is because we need the courage to receive feedback and we have to keep our 'ego' away to receive feedback. That's exactly the reason why we should have a good honest feedback partner. Most of the time improper approaches may result in frustrations, indifference, counter attack or even loss of relationships. Feedback is most required and should be in good taste. Sincerity and honesty in giving and receiving feedback will automatically be reciprocated when we are at the receiving end.

Characteristics of Giving Effective Feedback to an inner circle person.

- Focus on behaviour, not individual.

- Be focused on only the issue at hand.

- Timely: right place and as soon as possible. Praise in public. Criticise in private.

- Constructive: only for improvement and to be truthful.

- No Preaching.

- Validate: this should be realistic.

- Specific: precise language. Specify what was right and what went wrong. How they could have done better.

- Based on personal observation and not hearsay.

Characteristics of Receiving Effective Feedback from inner circle person.

- Be a good listener. This means not interrupting.

- Be open. Don`t be judgmental.

- Be aware of your responses especially your body language and tone of voice.

- Understand the message

- Reflect and take action

If we do not have a feedback partner, we would never know if we are going in the right direction, showingthe right behaviour, beingarrogant or aggressive was not necessary or takingthe right decision at crucial times.

I have seen many successful people in authority or even organizations who have fallen down in grace or in the eyes of people just because there was nobody to caution them at the right time or give them the most needed direction when needed.

These are the people who either did not have a feedback partner or felt that they never needed one. If the reason is the latter one "I do not need a feedback partner" then God help that person!

If we want to make things happen then we need to firmly believe that each one of us, at whatever position we are in our workplace, family or society must have a feedback partner.

Summary

Life-long learning is the 'ongoing, voluntary and self-motivated' pursuit of knowledge, skills and more importantly attitude for personal and professional reasons. Those who feel that they have 'learnt it all' fail to grow and thus stagnate. This book is meant for life-long learners.

Having been closely associated with academics forthe last 44 years, I have seen a lot of importance being given to imparting knowledge and developing skills of individuals during classroom teaching from nursery to higher education. Sadly, sharpening attitudinal skills, soft skills and relationship skills find no mention in their curriculum. These are the skills required later in life, post-education at the workplace, at home and in social circles.

Personal growth has always taken a back seat in our education system which has traditionally been focused on only 'passing' and moving on to the next grade assessing only the cognitive (knowledge) and psychomotor (skill) components of the individual.

This left us to develop our own attitudinal skills by observing people at home and in society or in association with the right or wrong kind of people. Some self-motivated individuals or those having mentors picked up self-help books or attended personal growth seminars and training programmes to sensitise their soft skills. The majority,however, never realised the importance of developing attitudinal skills till they had to face a situation that needed such skills.

There is an old saying 'If I had seven hours to chop a tree, I would spend five hours sharpening my axe'. For if my axe is sharp I could chop down the tree in just a few strokes.It's a life lesson and hence I ask,"When wasthe last time we sharpened our axe?" We are all busy in pursuit of growth and success in the family, workplace and social relationships, and spend less time sharpening our axe of life. Post our education, for professional reasons we do indulge in updating our knowledge and skill, but attitude takes a back seat.

Through this book, an attempt has been made to speak about twelve attributes that are essential for personal growth and if one is associated with them onecould realise phenomenal success. We always knew that these attributes existed and are important, but here we revisit them to refresh and rejuvenate ourselves.

Twelve basic principles to make things happen are as follows:

1. Positive perception or thinking that will lead to positive action or attitude. This is challenging since in 2022 we are expected to think positive in spite of all the odds or negativities around us.

2. Only people who keep their minds open can demonstrate adaptability or flexibility. If we want to cope with the speed and size of changes, we have to be adaptable. Only such people can demonstrate the above when they can identify habits that block their growth and move out of their comfort zones.

3. People who do their SWOT analysis regularly are more successful in life. A SWOT analysis is where we list down our (S) Strengths, (W) Weakness, (O) Create opportunities to convert our weakness into our strength, and work on the (T) Threats that accompany them. Converting weakness to strength involves three steps. First: see it or realise that it`s a weakness;second: accept it, andthird: do something about it.

4. Being ambitious is good. Dreaming is good. But only dreaming without action has no meaning. We have to plan and take action. We can create our own destiny if we follow these five steps

   a. Set clear goals. First long term goals and then break them down into small-term goals

   b. Focus on the short-term goals without losing sight of the long-term goal

   c. Identify and then minimise distractions

   d. Micro plan schedules and

   e. Act upon them

   Seven magic words of goal setting are as follows:

   Goals should be

   i. Challenging

   ii. Achievable

   iii. Specific

   iv. Dated

   v. Written

   vi. Reviewable with a

   vii. Burning desire

5. Accountability is when we take responsibility for our actions. Being accountable is an outcome of being disciplined in life. It's a virtue, a value that one can cherish all through our life. Disciplined persons do not need external motivation for every task that they undertake. Accountable people are also time conscious. When we respect others' time, we gain respect. One who does not value others' time will be slowly and gradually socially boycotted. If we like people to wait for us, then we are demonstrating "arrogance". Managing time is not so difficult since it's nothing but prioritizing activities. Today, timemanagement is a priority management.

6. Acceptability is when people like to speak to us, be with us and look for our company. And that is possible when we are approachable. Our body language demonstrates that we are people-centred; acceptable and approachable. Especially our facial expressions and voice modulation. Acceptability and Approachability are reflected when we have the ability to create a nonthreatening environment in any role that we play in life. One way of improving our acceptability is by joining social organizations where we are practically taught to work without arrogance and to shed our egos while working in a team with different types of people.

7. Creativity is doing the same thing differently. All of us have this ability, it's only that we have never trained our minds to think differently, to think out of the box. We are so busy with mundane things in a typically routine way that our thinking is restricted to only 'that' way. People who use this already existing ability outshine others, especially in competitive events or situations.

Everyone is born with some capabilities and an instinct to be successful, but only the ones who think differently and out of the box, succeed. Big ideas come from forward-thinking people who challenge the norm, think outside the box, and invent the world they see inside rather than submitting to the limitations of current dilemmas.

8. Extrovert and Introvert are two behaviours that we must have encountered around us at the workplace, at home or in social associations. We can choose to be an extrovert or an introvert depending on the situation. That's what professionalism is. If extrovert and introvert are two behaviours then ambivert is an ability. It is an ability to shift your behaviour from an extrovert to an introvert or vice versa depending on the situation without compromising on our core values. A person who has this ability is more acceptable. Others are comfortable working with such people. They are better team players and if required can emerge as better leaders.

9. Those who have this ability to express themselves or make powerful presentations have a definite edge over others. What good is the sea of contents when we cannot present our thoughts in a manner in which we can impress others? The knowledge unless expressed effectively is of no use. One of the basic necessities for any human being to excel is developing our presentation skills. Presentation is a skill and it can be learnt.

   There are four important steps while making a presentation.

   - Audience analysis

   - Designing and organizing the contents

   - Adding style to the presentation

   - Evaluating or looking for feedback

10. The most effective method to use while trying to accomplish our communication goal is the assertive approach.Several situations in life require us to be assertive. That is, being firm yet polite.

Especially in difficult situations with difficult people. Even in several common situations at home, workplace or in society we need to say 'NO' or 'Refuse' certain demands of peopleor make a point with people. This is where assertive communication helps. Expressing what you want to say 'without hurting people'. It also means letting people know what our priorities, preferences, wants, and needs are in a special situation while allowing them to state theirs and taking them into account.

Characteristics of assertive communication is a five-step approach

1. An appropriate openingin a **non-threatening environment**

2. Using receiver-friendly simple language with **rationality**

3. Understanding emotions (**empathy**)

4. **Assertive communication skills** with proper body language

5. Active **listening skills**

Four Things to Remember

- **How** we say is more important than **what** we want to say

- We may go to aggression or passivity depending on the situation and people. But don't get hooked on to them and quickly come back to assertion.

- To be assertive we need to create a non-threatening environment using rationality, empathy andactive listening.

- Assertiveness is a skill and it can be learnt and mastered.

1. Appreciating people for a job well done is a skill and an important attribute in personal growth and making people grow. It's a leadership skill to correctly assess which person or situation needs to be appreciated and more so 'how' to show appreciation. Organizational policies of rewards, recognitions and incentives go a long way in building trust and motivation among employees. This act of appreciation is applicable to everyone, to all people in any hierarchal position.

2. **The final question: Do we have a feedback partner?**

For all the eleven attributes to be a reality we need someone to tell us that we are going in the right direction. I call them feedback partners. Generally, feedback partners are people in our inner circle, who are our well-wishers and always want us to succeed. There is a mutual feeling of compassion towards each other. They do not fear reprimanding or appreciating us. Once we identify such persons as our feedback partners, we should nourish this relationship and never lose them as they shall be our valuable assets throughout our life. Each one of us, in whatever position we hold in our workplace, family or society always must have a feedback partner.

Don't wait for things to happen, make things happen.

About the Book

Personal growth which includes soft skills, attitudinal skills and relationship skills, has always taken a back seat in our education system. These are the skills required later in life, post-education at the workplace, at home and in social circles.

An attempt has been made in this book to elaborate on the twelve attributes that are essential for personal growth and for phenomenal success. These attributes always existed and this book revisits them to refresh and rejuvenate us.

The 12 attributes required to **make things happen** are as follows:

1. Attitude and Perception

2. Adaptability

3. Awareness about self

4. Ambitious with clear goals

5. Accountable (taking responsibility, disciplined and time conscious)

6. Acceptable and Approachable

7. Apart: Being creative and innovative

8. Ambivert: Ability to choose between extrovert and introvert behaviours depending on the situation

9. Active speaker

10. Assertive communication with rationality and empathy

11. Appreciation

12. And finally: Do we have a feedback partner?

About The Author, Dr Suresh Chari is a well-known Corporate Trainer, Soft Skills Trainer, Life Coach and Motivator. He has been a professor, teaching biochemistry in various medical colleges in Maharashtra, India since last 44 years.

Being a psychological counselor, he has been actively involved in shaping the personality of thousands of participants since 1990. "Don't wait for things to happen, make things happen. Be the architect of your own life design" is the strong and clear message he sends to them in all his training programmes.

He is regularly associated with several business houses for corporate training on leadership, team building, managing relationships, communication skills, self-concept, public speaking and presentation skills and training of trainer's workshops.

Dr Chari is the most sought-after trainer by various social organizations, schools, colleges and chartered accountant institutes for conducting soft skill development programmes including group discussion and interview skills. He has been a regular faculty at the Center of Excellence of ICAI at Hyderabad and Jaipur.

Dr Suresh Chari is known for his powerful oratory and communication skills, his very simple, lucid and easy blend of English and Hindi, and a body language that can be understood and appreciated by everyone. Humour and real-life examples make him reach out to all.